MW01075359

PUBLISHER COMMENT

This PRINT REPLICA is the **SEC Regulation S-X** and is current to **JULY 5, 2018**.

Regulation S-X is a prescribed regulation in the United States of America that lays out the specific form and content of financial reports, specifically the financial statements of public companies. Also known as the **"FORM AND CONTENT OF AND REQUIREMENTS FOR FINANCIAL STATEMENTS, SECURITIES ACT OF 1933, SECURITIES EXCHANGE ACT OF 1934, INVESTMENT COMPANY ACT OF 1940, INVESTMENT ADVISERS ACT OF 1940, AND ENERGY POLICY AND CONSERVATION ACT OF 1975."** Regulation S-X and the Financial Reporting Releases set forth the form and content of and requirements for financial statements required to be filed as a part of a registration statements under the Securities Act of 1933. Regulation S-X extends the meaning of the term 'financial statements' to include all notes to the statements and all related schedules. Regulation S-X is closely related to Regulation S-K, which lays out reporting requirements for various SEC filings and registrations used by public companies.

Why buy a hard copy book you can download for free?

We print this so you don't have to.

Anyone that has worked in securities knows how difficult it is to search for that one bit of information that will make or break a deal. Many people need glasses to read and don't like books with small print. That's especially true of complex technical subjects like acquisition regulations. We print the hard copy books a full 8 ½ inches by 11 inches, with large text. There are also wide margins so you can jot down notes.

You could print a 1,900-page book over the network, punch holes and put it in a humongous binder, but it's not cost effective. A contracting officer that's paid $75 an hour has to do this using a printer shared with 100 other people – and it's out of paper, and the toner is low. It's much easier to order a copy at Amazon.com

This material is published by 4th Watch Publishing Co. We publish tightly-bound, full-size books at 8 ½ by 11 inches, with large text and glossy covers. 4th Watch Publishing Co. is a Service Disabled Veteran Owned Small Business (SDVOSB). Please visit www.usgovpub.com.

Other books we publish that are available on Amazon.com include:

SEC	Exchange Traded Funds New Rules	June 2018
SEC	Prohibitions and Restrictions on Proprietary Trading and Certain Interests in, and Relationships With, Hedge Funds and Private Equity Funds	June 2018
SEC	Financial Reporting Manual	December 2017
SEC	Rules of Practice	June 2018
SEC	How to Create Clear SEC Disclosure Documents	
Dept of Justice	Antitrust Division Manual	August 2017
GAO	Principles of Federal Appropriations Law	
GAO FAM	GAO Financial Audit Manual	
GAO-01-1008G	Internal Control Management and Evaluation Tool	
GAO-17-313SP	Government Auditing Standards (Yellow Book)	
GAO-14-704G	Standards for Internal Control in the Federal Government (Green Book)	
GAO-16-410G	Technology Readiness Assessment Guide	Aug-16
GAO-09-3SP	Cost Estimating and Assessment Guide	Mar-09
GAO-16-89G	GAO Schedule Assessment Guide	Dec-15
FISCAM	Federal Information System Controls Audit Manual	
OMB A-123	Management's Responsibility for Enterprise Risk Management and Internal Control	
FISMA	Federal Information Security Modernization Act & OMB A-130	
FY19 Budget	Budget of the U.S. Government	
FITARA	Federal Information Technology Acquisition Reform	

Federal Rules of Appellate Procedure (2017)
Federal Rules of Rules of Criminal Procedure (2017)
Federal Rules of Rules of Civil Procedure (2017)
Federal Rules of Rules of Bankruptcy Procedure (2017)
Benchbook for U.S. District Court Judges (2013)
Military Judges' Benchbook (2017)
Principles of Federal Appropriations Law 4th Edition
Immigration Court Practice Manual
DoD Law of War Manual (2016)
DoD Operational Law Handbook (2017)
DoD Domestic Operational Law Handbook (2015)
DoD Rule of Law Handbook (2015)
Manual de Práctica de la Corte de Inmigración (2017)

SEC Regulation S-X

FORM AND CONTENT OF AND REQUIREMENTS FOR
FINANCIAL STATEMENTS, SECURITIES ACT OF 1933,
SECURITIES EXCHANGE ACT OF 1934, INVESTMENT
COMPANY ACT OF 1940, INVESTMENT ADVISERS ACT OF
1940, AND ENERGY POLICY AND CONSERVATION ACT OF
1975

Title 17 → Chapter II → Part 210

Title 17: Commodity and Securities Exchanges

Electronic Code of Federal Regulations
e-CFR data is current as of July 5, 2018

Table of Contents

Authority: 15 U.S.C. 77f, 77g, 77h, 77j, 77s, 77z-2, 77z-3, 77aa(25), 77aa(26), 77nn(25), 77nn(26), 78c, 78j-1, 78l, 78m, 78n, 78o(d), 78q, 78u-5, 78w, 78ll, 78mm, 80a-8, 80a-20, 80a-29, 80a-30, 80a-31, 80a-37(a), 80b-3, 80b-11, 7202 and 7262, and sec. 102(c), Pub. L. 112-106, 126 Stat. 310 (2012), unless otherwise noted.

ATTENTION ELECTRONIC FILERS
THIS REGULATION SHOULD BE READ IN CONJUNCTION WITH REGULATION S-T (PART 232 OF THIS CHAPTER), WHICH GOVERNS THE PREPARATION AND SUBMISSION OF DOCUMENTS IN ELECTRONIC FORMAT. MANY PROVISIONS RELATING TO THE PREPARATION AND SUBMISSION OF DOCUMENTS IN PAPER FORMAT CONTAINED IN THIS REGULATION ARE SUPERSEDED BY THE PROVISIONS OF REGULATION S-T FOR DOCUMENTS REQUIRED TO BE FILED IN ELECTRONIC FORMAT.

Application of Regulation S-X (17 CFR Part 210)

§210.1-01   Application of Regulation S-X (17 CFR part 210).

(a) This part (together with the Financial Reporting Releases (part 211 of this chapter)) sets forth the form and content of and requirements for financial statements required to be filed as a part of:

(1) Registration statements under the Securities Act of 1933 (part 239 of this chapter), except as otherwise specifically provided in the forms which are to be used for registration under this Act;

(2) Registration statements under section 12 (subpart C of part 249 of this chapter), annual or other reports under sections 13 and 15(d) (subparts D and E of part 249 of this chapter), and proxy and information statements under section 14 of the Securities Exchange Act of 1934 except as otherwise specifically provided in the forms which are to be used for registration and reporting under these sections of this Act; and

(3) Registration statements and shareholder reports under the Investment Company Act of 1940 (part 274 of this chapter), except as otherwise specifically provided in the forms which are to be used for registration under this Act.

(b) The term financial statements as used in this part shall be deemed to include all notes to the statements and all related schedules.

(c) In addition to filings pursuant to the Federal securities laws, §210.4-10 applies to the preparation of accounts by persons engaged, in whole or in part, in the production of crude oil or natural gas in the United States pursuant to section 503 of the Energy Policy and Conservation Act of 1975 (42 U.S.C. 6383) (EPCA) and section 1(c) of the Energy Supply and Environmental Coordination Act of 1974 (15 U.S.C. 796), as amended by section 505 of EPCA.

[37 FR 14593, July 21, 1972, as amended at 43 FR 40712, Sept. 12, 1978; 45 FR 63680, 63687, Sept. 25, 1980; 46 FR 36124, July 14, 1981; 50 FR 25214, June 18, 1985; 76 FR 71875, Nov. 21, 2011]

§210.1-02   Definitions of terms used in Regulation S-X (17 CFR part 210).

Unless the context otherwise requires, terms defined in the general rules and regulations or in the instructions to the applicable form, when used in Regulation S-X (this part 210), shall have the respective meanings given in such instructions or rules. In addition, the following terms shall have the meanings indicated in this section unless the context otherwise requires.

(a)(1) Accountant's report. The term accountant's report, when used in regard to financial statements, means a document in which an independent public or certified public accountant indicates the scope of the audit (or examination) which he has made and sets forth his opinion regarding the financial statements taken as a whole, or an assertion to the effect that an overall

1

opinion cannot be expressed. When an overall opinion cannot be expressed, the reasons therefor shall be stated.

(2) Attestation report on internal control over financial reporting. The term attestation report on internal control over financial reporting means a report in which a registered public accounting firm expresses an opinion, either unqualified or adverse, as to whether the registrant maintained, in all material respects, effective internal control over financial reporting (as defined in §240.13a-15(f) or §240.15d-15(f) of this chapter), except in the rare circumstance of a scope limitation that cannot be overcome by the registrant or the registered public accounting firm which would result in the accounting firm disclaiming an opinion.

(3) Attestation report on assessment of compliance with servicing criteria for asset-backed securities. The term attestation report on assessment of compliance with servicing criteria for asset-backed securities means a report in which a registered public accounting firm, as required by §240.13a-18(c) or §240.15d-18(c) of this chapter, expresses an opinion, or states that an opinion cannot be expressed, concerning an asserting party's assessment of compliance with servicing criteria, as required by §240.13a-18(b) or §240.15d-18(b) of this chapter, in accordance with standards on attestation engagements. When an overall opinion cannot be expressed, the registered public accounting firm must state why it is unable to express such an opinion.

(4) Definitions of terms related to internal control over financial reporting.

Material weakness means a deficiency, or a combination of deficiencies, in internal control over financial reporting (as defined in §240.13a-15(f) or §240.15d-15(f) of this chapter) such that there is a reasonable possibility that a material misstatement of the registrant's annual or interim financial statements will not be prevented or detected on a timely basis.

Significant deficiency means a deficiency, or a combination of deficiencies, in internal control over financial reporting that is less severe than a material weakness, yet important enough to merit attention by those responsible for oversight of the registrant's financial reporting.

(b) Affiliate. An affiliate of, or a person affiliated with, a specific person is a person that directly, or indirectly through one or more intermediaries, controls, or is controlled by, or is under common control with, the person specified.

(c) Amount. The term amount, when used in regard to securities, means the principal amount if relating to evidences of indebtedness, the number of shares if relating to shares, and the number of units if relating to any other kind of security.

(d) Audit (or examination). The term audit (or examination), when used in regard to financial statements, means an examination of the financial statements by an independent accountant in accordance with generally accepted auditing standards, as may be modified or supplemented by the Commission, for the purpose of expressing an opinion thereon.

(e) Bank holding company. The term bank holding company means a person which is engaged, either directly or indirectly, primarily in the business of owning securities of one or more banks for the purpose, and with the effect, of exercising control.

(f) Certified. The term certified, when used in regard to financial statements, means examined and reported upon with an opinion expressed by an independent public or certified public accountant.

(g) Control. The term control (including the terms controlling, controlled by and under common control with) means the possession, direct or indirect, of the power to direct or cause the direction of the management and policies of a person, whether through the ownership of voting shares, by contract, or otherwise.

(h) Development stage company. A company shall be considered to be in the development stage if it is devoting substantially all of its efforts to establishing a new business and either of the following conditions exists: (1) Planned principal operations have not commenced. (2) Planned principal operations have commenced, but there has been no significant revenue therefrom.

(i) Equity security. The term equity security means any stock or similar security; or any security convertible, with or without consideration, into such a security, or carrying any warrant or right to subscribe to or purchase such a security; or any such warrant or right.

(j) Fifty-percent-owned person. The term 50-percent-owned person, in relation to a specified person, means a person approximately 50 percent of whose outstanding voting shares is owned by the specified person either directly, or indirectly through one or more intermediaries.

(k) Fiscal year. The term fiscal year means the annual accounting period or, if no closing date has been adopted, the calendar year ending on December 31.

(l) Foreign business. A business that is majority owned by persons who are not citizens or residents of the United States and is not organized under the laws of the United States or any state thereof, and either:

(1) More than 50 percent of its assets are located outside the United States; or

(2) The majority of its executive officers and directors are not United States citizens or residents.

(m) Insurance holding company. The term insurance holding company means a person which is engaged, either directly or indirectly, primarily in the business of owning securities of one or more insurance companies for the purpose, and with the effect, of exercising control.

(n) Majority-owned subsidiary. The term majority-owned subsidiary means a subsidiary more than 50 percent of whose outstanding voting shares is owned by its parent and/or the parent's other majority-owned subsidiaries.

(o) Material. The term material, when used to qualify a requirement for the furnishing of information as to any subject, limits the information required to those matters about which an average prudent investor ought reasonably to be informed.

(p) Parent. A parent of a specified person is an affiliate controlling such person directly, or indirectly through one or more intermediaries.

(q) Person. The term person means an individual, a corporation, a partnership, an association, a joint-stock company, a business trust, or an unincorporated organization.

(r) Principal holder of equity securities. The term principal holder of equity securities, used in respect of a registrant or other person named in a particular statement or report, means a holder of record or a known beneficial owner of more than 10 percent of any class of equity securities of the registrant or other person, respectively, as of the date of the related balance sheet filed.

(s) Promoter. The term promoter includes:

(1) Any person who, acting alone or in conjunction with one or more other persons, directly or indirectly takes initiative in founding and organizing the business or enterprise of an issuer;

(2) Any person who, in connection with the founding and organizing of the business or enterprise of an issuer, directly or indirectly receives in consideration of services or property, or both services and property, 10 percent or more of any class of securities of the issuer or 10 percent or more of the proceeds from the sale of any class of securities. However, a person who receives such securities or proceeds either solely as underwriting commissions or solely in consideration of property shall not be deemed a promoter within the meaning of this paragraph if such person does not otherwise take part in founding and organizing the enterprise.

(t) Registrant. The term registrant means the issuer of the securities for which an application, a registration statement, or a report is filed.

(u) Related parties. The term related parties is used as that term is defined in the FASB ASC Master Glossary.

(v) Share. The term share means a share of stock in a corporation or unit of interest in an unincorporated person.

(w) Significant subsidiary. The term significant subsidiary means a subsidiary, including its subsidiaries, which meets any of the following conditions:

(1) The registrant's and its other subsidiaries' investments in and advances to the subsidiary exceed 10 percent of the total assets of the registrant and its subsidiaries consolidated as of the end of the most recently completed fiscal year (for a proposed combination between entities under common control, this condition is also met when the number of common shares exchanged or to be exchanged by the registrant exceeds 10 percent of its total common shares outstanding at the date the combination is initiated); or

(2) The registrant's and its other subsidiaries' proportionate share of the total assets (after intercompany eliminations) of the subsidiary exceeds 10 percent of the total assets of the registrants and its subsidiaries consolidated as of the end of the most recently completed fiscal year; or

(3) The registrant's and its other subsidiaries' equity in the income from continuing operations before income taxes, extraordinary items and cumulative effect of a change in accounting principle of the subsidiary exclusive of amounts attributable to any noncontrolling interests exceeds 10 percent of such income of the registrant and its subsidiaries consolidated for the most recently completed fiscal year.

Note to paragraph (w): A registrant that files its financial statements in accordance with or provides a reconciliation to U.S. Generally Accepted Accounting Principles shall make the prescribed tests using amounts determined under U.S. Generally Accepted Accounting Principles. A foreign private issuer that files its financial statements in accordance with IFRS as issued by the IASB shall make the prescribed tests using amounts determined under IFRS as issued by the IASB.

Computational note: For purposes of making the prescribed income test the following guidance should be applied:

1. When a loss exclusive of amounts attributable to any noncontrolling interests has been incurred by either the parent and its subsidiaries consolidated or the tested subsidiary, but not both, the equity in the income or loss of the tested subsidiary exclusive of amounts attributable to any noncontrolling interests should be excluded from such income of the registrant and its subsidiaries consolidated for purposes of the computation.

2. If income of the registrant and its subsidiaries consolidated exclusive of amounts attributable to any noncontrolling interests for the most recent fiscal year is at least 10 percent lower than the average of the income for the last five fiscal years, such average income should be submitted for purposes of the computation. Any loss years should be omitted for purposes of computing average income.

3. Where the test involves combined entities, as in the case of determining whether summarized financial data should be presented, entities reporting losses shall not be aggregated with entities reporting income.

(x) Subsidiary. A subsidiary of a specified person is an affiliate controlled by such person directly, or indirectly through one or more intermediaries.

(y) Totally held subsidiary. The term totally held subsidiary means a subsidiary (1) substantially all of whose outstanding equity securities are owned by its parent and/or the parent's other totally held subsidiaries, and (2) which is not indebted to any person other than its parent and/or the parent's other totally held subsidiaries, in an amount which is material in relation to the particular subsidiary, excepting indebtedness incurred in the ordinary course of business which is not overdue and which matures within 1 year from the date of its creation, whether evidenced by securities or not. Indebtedness of a subsidiary which is secured by its parent by guarantee, pledge, assignment, or otherwise is to be excluded for purposes of paragraph (x)(2) of this section.

(z) Voting shares. The term voting shares means the sum of all rights, other than as affected by events of default, to vote for election of directors and/or the sum of all interests in an unincorporated person.

(aa) Wholly owned subsidiary. The term wholly owned subsidiary means a subsidiary substantially all of whose outstanding voting shares are owned by its parent and/or the parent's other wholly owned subsidiaries.

(bb) Summarized financial information. (1) Except as provided in paragraph (aa)(2), summarized financial information referred to in this regulation shall mean the presentation of summarized information as to the assets, liabilities and results of operations of the entity for which the information is required. Summarized financial information shall include the following disclosures:

(i) Current assets, noncurrent assets, current liabilities, noncurrent liabilities, and, when applicable, redeemable preferred stocks (see §210.5-02.27) and noncontrolling interests (for specialized industries in which classified balance sheets are normally not presented, information shall be provided as to the nature and amount of the majority components of assets and liabilities);

(ii) Net sales or gross revenues, gross profit (or, alternatively, costs and expenses applicable to net sales or gross revenues), income or loss from continuing operations before extraordinary items and cumulative effect of a change in accounting principle, net income or loss, and net income or loss attributable to the entity (for specialized industries, other information may be substituted for sales and related costs and expenses if necessary for a more meaningful presentation); and

(2) Summarized financial information for unconsolidated subsidiaries and 50 percent or less owned persons referred to in and required by §210.10-01(b) for interim periods shall include the information required by paragraph (aa)(1)(ii) of this section.

[37 FR 14593, July 21, 1972]

Editorial Note: For Federal Register citations affecting §210.1-02, see the List of CFR Sections Affected, which appears in the Finding Aids section of the printed volume and at www.fdsys.gov.

Qualifications and Reports of Accountants
Source: Sections 210.2-01 through 210.2-05 appear at 37 FR 14594, July 21, 1972, unless otherwise noted.

§210.2-01 Qualifications of accountants.

Preliminary Note to §210.2-01

1. Section 210.2-01 is designed to ensure that auditors are qualified and independent of their audit clients both in fact and in appearance. Accordingly, the rule sets forth restrictions on financial, employment, and business relationships between an accountant and an audit client and restrictions on an accountant providing certain non-audit services to an audit client.

2. Section 210.2-01(b) sets forth the general standard of auditor independence. Paragraphs (c)(1) to (c)(5) reflect the application of the general standard to particular circumstances. The rule does not purport to, and the Commission could not, consider all circumstances that raise independence concerns, and these are subject to the general standard in §210.2-01(b). In considering this standard, the Commission looks in the first instance to whether a relationship or the provision of a service: creates a mutual or conflicting interest between the accountant and the audit client; places the accountant in the position of auditing his or her own work; results in the accountant acting as management or an employee of the audit client; or places the accountant in a position of being an advocate for the audit client.

3. These factors are general guidance only and their application may depend on particular facts and circumstances. For that reason, §210.2-01 provides that, in determining whether an accountant is independent, the Commission will consider all relevant facts and circumstances. For the same reason, registrants and accountants are encouraged to consult with the Commission's Office of the Chief Accountant before entering into relationships, including relationships involving the provision of services, that are not explicitly described in the rule.

(a) The Commission will not recognize any person as a certified public accountant who is not duly registered and in good standing as such under the laws of the place of his residence or principal office. The Commission will not recognize any person as a public accountant who is not in good standing and entitled to practice as such under the laws of the place of his residence or principal office.

(b) The Commission will not recognize an accountant as independent, with respect to an audit client, if the accountant is not, or a reasonable investor with knowledge of all relevant facts and circumstances would conclude that the accountant is not, capable of exercising objective and impartial judgment on all issues encompassed within the accountant's engagement. In determining whether an accountant is independent, the Commission will consider all relevant circumstances, including all relationships between the accountant and the audit client, and not just those relating to reports filed with the Commission.

(c) This paragraph sets forth a non-exclusive specification of circumstances inconsistent with paragraph (b) of this section.

(1) Financial relationships. An accountant is not independent if, at any point during the audit and professional engagement period, the accountant has a direct financial interest or a material indirect financial interest in the accountant's audit client, such as:

(i) Investments in audit clients. An accountant is not independent when:

(A) The accounting firm, any covered person in the firm, or any of his or her immediate family members, has any direct investment in an audit client, such as stocks, bonds, notes, options, or other securities. The term direct investment includes an investment in an audit client through an intermediary if:

(1) The accounting firm, covered person, or immediate family member, alone or together with other persons, supervises or participates in the intermediary's investment decisions or has control over the intermediary; or

(2) The intermediary is not a diversified management investment company, as defined by section 5(b)(1) of the Investment Company Act of 1940, 15 U.S.C. 80a-5(b)(1), and has an investment in the audit client that amounts to 20% or more of the value of the intermediary's total investments.

(B) Any partner, principal, shareholder, or professional employee of the accounting firm, any of his or her immediate family members, any close family member of a covered person in the firm, or any group of the above persons has filed a Schedule 13D or 13G (17 CFR 240.13d-101 or 240.13d-102) with the Commission indicating beneficial ownership of more than five percent of an audit client's equity securities or controls an audit client, or a close family member of a partner, principal, or shareholder of the accounting firm controls an audit client.

(C) The accounting firm, any covered person in the firm, or any of his or her immediate family members, serves as voting trustee of a trust, or executor of an estate, containing the securities of an audit client, unless the accounting firm, covered person in the firm, or immediate family member has no authority to make investment decisions for the trust or estate.

(D) The accounting firm, any covered person in the firm, any of his or her immediate family members, or any group of the above persons has any material indirect investment in an audit client. For purposes of this paragraph, the term material indirect investment does not include ownership by any covered person in the firm, any of his or her immediate family members, or any group of the above persons of 5% or less of the outstanding shares of a diversified management investment company, as defined by section 5(b)(1) of the Investment Company Act of 1940, 15 U.S.C. 80a-5(b)(1), that invests in an audit client.

(E) The accounting firm, any covered person in the firm, or any of his or her immediate family members:

(1) Has any direct or material indirect investment in an entity where:

(i) An audit client has an investment in that entity that is material to the audit client and has the ability to exercise significant influence over that entity; or

(ii) The entity has an investment in an audit client that is material to that entity and has the ability to exercise significant influence over that audit client;

(2) Has any material investment in an entity over which an audit client has the ability to exercise significant influence; or

(3) Has the ability to exercise significant influence over an entity that has the ability to exercise significant influence over an audit client.

(ii) Other financial interests in audit client. An accountant is not independent when the accounting firm, any covered person in the firm, or any of his or her immediate family members has:

(A) Loans/debtor-creditor relationship. Any loan (including any margin loan) to or from an audit client, or an audit client's officers, directors, or record or beneficial owners of more than ten percent of the audit client's equity securities, except for the following loans obtained from a financial institution under its normal lending procedures, terms, and requirements:

(1) Automobile loans and leases collateralized by the automobile;

(2) Loans fully collateralized by the cash surrender value of an insurance policy;

(3) Loans fully collateralized by cash deposits at the same financial institution; and

(4) A mortgage loan collateralized by the borrower's primary residence provided the loan was not obtained while the covered person in the firm was a covered person.

(B) Savings and checking accounts. Any savings, checking, or similar account at a bank, savings and loan, or similar institution that is an audit client, if the account has a balance that exceeds the amount insured by the Federal Deposit Insurance Corporation or any similar insurer, except that an accounting firm account may have an uninsured balance provided that the likelihood of the bank, savings and loan, or similar institution experiencing financial difficulties is remote.

(C) Broker-dealer accounts. Brokerage or similar accounts maintained with a broker-dealer that is an audit client, if:

(1) Any such account includes any asset other than cash or securities (within the meaning of "security" provided in the Securities Investor Protection Act of 1970 ("SIPA") (15 U.S.C. 78aaa et seq.));

(2) The value of assets in the accounts exceeds the amount that is subject to a Securities Investor Protection Corporation advance, for those accounts, under Section 9 of SIPA (15 U.S.C. 78fff-3); or

(3) With respect to non-U.S. accounts not subject to SIPA protection, the value of assets in the accounts exceeds the amount insured or protected by a program similar to SIPA.

(D) Futures commission merchant accounts. Any futures, commodity, or similar account maintained with a futures commission merchant that is an audit client.

(E) Credit cards. Any aggregate outstanding credit card balance owed to a lender that is an audit client that is not reduced to $10,000 or less on a current basis taking into consideration the payment due date and any available grace period.

(F) Insurance products. Any individual policy issued by an insurer that is an audit client unless:

(1) The policy was obtained at a time when the covered person in the firm was not a covered person in the firm; and

(2) The likelihood of the insurer becoming insolvent is remote.

(G) Investment companies. Any financial interest in an entity that is part of an investment company complex that includes an audit client.

(iii) Exceptions. Notwithstanding paragraphs (c)(1)(i) and (c)(1)(ii) of this section, an accountant will not be deemed not independent if:

(A) Inheritance and gift. Any person acquires an unsolicited financial interest, such as through an unsolicited gift or inheritance, that would cause an accountant to be not independent under paragraph (c)(1)(i) or (c)(1)(ii) of this section, and the financial interest is disposed of as soon as practicable, but no later than 30 days after the person has knowledge of and the right to dispose of the financial interest.

(B) New audit engagement. Any person has a financial interest that would cause an accountant to be not independent under paragraph (c)(1)(i) or (c)(1)(ii) of this section, and:

(1) The accountant did not audit the client's financial statements for the immediately preceding fiscal year; and

(2) The accountant is independent under paragraph (c)(1)(i) and (c)(1)(ii) of this section before the earlier of:

(i) Signing an initial engagement letter or other agreement to provide audit, review, or attest services to the audit client; or

(ii) Commencing any audit, review, or attest procedures (including planning the audit of the client's financial statements).

(C) Employee compensation and benefit plans. An immediate family member of a person who is a covered person in the firm only by virtue of paragraphs (f)(11)(iii) or (f)(11)(iv) of this section has a financial interest that would cause an accountant to be not independent under paragraph (c)(1)(i) or (c)(1)(ii) of this section, and the acquisition of the financial interest was an unavoidable consequence of participation in his or her employer's employee compensation or benefits program, provided that the financial interest, other than unexercised employee stock options, is disposed of as soon as practicable, but no later than 30 days after the person has the right to dispose of the financial interest.

(iv) Audit clients' financial relationships. An accountant is not independent when:

(A) Investments by the audit client in the accounting firm. An audit client has, or has agreed to acquire, any direct investment in the accounting firm, such as stocks, bonds, notes, options, or other securities, or the audit client's officers or directors are record or beneficial owners of more than 5% of the equity securities of the accounting firm.

(B) Underwriting. An accounting firm engages an audit client to act as an underwriter, broker-dealer, market-maker, promoter, or analyst with respect to securities issued by the accounting firm.

(2) Employment relationships. An accountant is not independent if, at any point during the audit and professional engagement period, the accountant has an employment relationship with an audit client, such as:

(i) Employment at audit client of accountant. A current partner, principal, shareholder, or professional employee of the accounting firm is employed by the audit client or serves as a member of the board of directors or similar management or governing body of the audit client.

(ii) Employment at audit client of certain relatives of accountant. A close family member of a covered person in the firm is in an accounting role or financial reporting oversight role at an audit client, or was in such a role during any period covered by an audit for which the covered person in the firm is a covered person.

(iii) Employment at audit client of former employee of accounting firm. (A) A former partner, principal, shareholder, or professional employee of an accounting firm is in an accounting role or financial reporting oversight role at an audit client, unless the individual:

(1) Does not influence the accounting firm's operations or financial policies;

(2) Has no capital balances in the accounting firm; and

(3) Has no financial arrangement with the accounting firm other than one providing for regular payment of a fixed dollar amount (which is not dependent on the revenues, profits, or earnings of the accounting firm):

(i) Pursuant to a fully funded retirement plan, rabbi trust, or, in jurisdictions in which a rabbi trust does not exist, a similar vehicle; or

(ii) In the case of a former professional employee who was not a partner, principal, or shareholder of the accounting firm and who has been disassociated from the accounting firm for more than five years, that is immaterial to the former professional employee; and

(B) A former partner, principal, shareholder, or professional employee of an accounting firm is in a financial reporting oversight role at an issuer (as defined in section 10A(f) of the Securities Exchange Act of 1934 (15 U.S.C. 78j-1(f)), except an issuer that is an investment company registered under section 8 of the Investment Company Act of 1940 (15 U.S.C. 80a-8), unless the individual:

(1) Employed by the issuer was not a member of the audit engagement team of the issuer during the one year period preceding the date that audit procedures commenced for the fiscal period that included the date of initial employment of the audit engagement team member by the issuer;

(2) For purposes of paragraph (c)(2)(iii)(B)(1) of this section, the following individuals are not considered to be members of the audit engagement team:

(i) Persons, other than the lead partner and the concurring partner, who provided ten or fewer hours of audit, review, or attest services during the period covered by paragraph (c)(2)(iii)(B)(1) of this section;

(ii) Individuals employed by the issuer as a result of a business combination between an issuer that is an audit client and the employing entity, provided employment was not in contemplation of the business combination and the audit committee of the successor issuer is aware of the prior employment relationship; and

(iii) Individuals that are employed by the issuer due to an emergency or other unusual situation provided that the audit committee determines that the relationship is in the interest of investors;

(3) For purposes of paragraph (c)(2)(iii)(B)(1) of this section, audit procedures are deemed to have commenced for a fiscal period the day following the filing of the issuer's periodic annual report with the Commission covering the previous fiscal period; or

(C) A former partner, principal, shareholder, or professional employee of an accounting firm is in a financial reporting oversight role with respect to an investment company registered under section 8 of the Investment Company Act of 1940 (15 U.S.C. 80a-8), if:

(1) The former partner, principal, shareholder, or professional employee of an accounting firm is employed in a financial reporting oversight role related to the operations and financial reporting of the registered investment company at an entity in the investment company complex, as defined in (f)(14) of this section, that includes the registered investment company; and

(2) The former partner, principal, shareholder, or professional employee of an accounting firm employed by the registered investment company or any entity in the investment company complex was a member of the audit engagement team of the registered investment company or any other registered investment company in the investment company complex during the one

year period preceding the date that audit procedures commenced that included the date of initial employment of the audit engagement team member by the registered investment company or any entity in the investment company complex.

(3) For purposes of paragraph (c)(2)(iii)(C)(2) of this section, the following individuals are not considered to be members of the audit engagement team:

(i) Persons, other than the lead partner and concurring partner, who provided ten or fewer hours of audit, review or attest services during the period covered by paragraph (c)(2)(iii)(C)(2) of this section;

(ii) Individuals employed by the registered investment company or any entity in the investment company complex as a result of a business combination between a registered investment company or any entity in the investment company complex that is an audit client and the employing entity, provided employment was not in contemplation of the business combination and the audit committee of the registered investment company is aware of the prior employment relationship; and

(iii) Individuals that are employed by the registered investment company or any entity in the investment company complex due to an emergency or other unusual situation provided that the audit committee determines that the relationship is in the interest of investors.

(4) For purposes of paragraph (c)(2)(iii)(C)(2) of this section, audit procedures are deemed to have commenced the day following the filing of the registered investment company's periodic annual report with the Commission.

(iv) Employment at accounting firm of former employee of audit client. A former officer, director, or employee of an audit client becomes a partner, principal, shareholder, or professional employee of the accounting firm, unless the individual does not participate in, and is not in a position to influence, the audit of the financial statements of the audit client covering any period during which he or she was employed by or associated with that audit client.

(3) Business relationships. An accountant is not independent if, at any point during the audit and professional engagement period, the accounting firm or any covered person in the firm has any direct or material indirect business relationship with an audit client, or with persons associated with the audit client in a decision-making capacity, such as an audit client's officers, directors, or substantial stockholders. The relationships described in this paragraph do not include a relationship in which the accounting firm or covered person in the firm provides professional services to an audit client or is a consumer in the ordinary course of business.

(4) Non-audit services. An accountant is not independent if, at any point during the audit and professional engagement period, the accountant provides the following non-audit services to an audit client:

(i) Bookkeeping or other services related to the accounting records or financial statements of the audit client. Any service, unless it is reasonable to conclude that the results of these services will not be subject to audit procedures during an audit of the audit client's financial statements, including:

(A) Maintaining or preparing the audit client's accounting records;

(B) Preparing the audit client's financial statements that are filed with the Commission or that form the basis of financial statements filed with the Commission; or

(C) Preparing or originating source data underlying the audit client's financial statements.

(ii) Financial information systems design and implementation. Any service, unless it is reasonable to conclude that the results of these services will not be subject to audit procedures during an audit of the audit client's financial statements, including:

(A) Directly or indirectly operating, or supervising the operation of, the audit client's information system or managing the audit client's local area network; or

(B) Designing or implementing a hardware or software system that aggregates source data underlying the financial statements or generates information that is significant to the audit client's financial statements or other financial information systems taken as a whole.

(iii) Appraisal or valuation services, fairness opinions, or contribution-in-kind reports. Any appraisal service, valuation service, or any service involving a fairness opinion or contribution-in-kind report for an audit client, unless it is reasonable to conclude that the results of these services will not be subject to audit procedures during an audit of the audit client's financial statements.

(iv) Actuarial services. Any actuarially-oriented advisory service involving the determination of amounts recorded in the financial statements and related accounts for the audit client other than assisting a client in understanding the methods, models, assumptions, and inputs used in computing an amount, unless it is reasonable to conclude that the results of these services will not be subject to audit procedures during an audit of the audit client's financial statements.

(v) Internal audit outsourcing services. Any internal audit service that has been outsourced by the audit client that relates to the audit client's internal accounting controls, financial systems, or financial statements, for an audit client unless it is reasonable to conclude that the results of these services will not be subject to audit procedures during an audit of the audit client's financial statements.

(vi) Management functions. Acting, temporarily or permanently, as a director, officer, or employee of an audit client, or performing any decision-making, supervisory, or ongoing monitoring function for the audit client.

(vii) Human resources. (A) Searching for or seeking out prospective candidates for managerial, executive, or director positions;

(B) Engaging in psychological testing, or other formal testing or evaluation programs;

(C) Undertaking reference checks of prospective candidates for an executive or director position;

(D) Acting as a negotiator on the audit client's behalf, such as determining position, status or title, compensation, fringe benefits, or other conditions of employment; or

(E) Recommending, or advising the audit client to hire, a specific candidate for a specific job (except that an accounting firm may, upon request by the audit client, interview candidates and advise the audit client on the candidate's competence for financial accounting, administrative, or control positions).

(viii) Broker-dealer, investment adviser, or investment banking services. Acting as a broker-dealer (registered or unregistered), promoter, or underwriter, on behalf of an audit client, making investment decisions on behalf of the audit client or otherwise having discretionary authority over an audit client's investments, executing a transaction to buy or sell an audit client's investment, or having custody of assets of the audit client, such as taking temporary possession of securities purchased by the audit client.

(ix) Legal services. Providing any service to an audit client that, under circumstances in which the service is provided, could be provided only by someone licensed, admitted, or otherwise qualified to practice law in the jurisdiction in which the service is provided.

(x) Expert services unrelated to the audit. Providing an expert opinion or other expert service for an audit client, or an audit client's legal representative, for the purpose of advocating an audit client's interests in litigation or in a regulatory or administrative proceeding or investigation. In any litigation or regulatory or administrative proceeding or investigation, an accountant's independence shall not be deemed to be impaired if the accountant provides factual accounts, including in testimony, of work performed or explains the positions taken or conclusions reached during the performance of any service provided by the accountant for the audit client.

(5) Contingent fees. An accountant is not independent if, at any point during the audit and professional engagement period, the accountant provides any service or product to an audit client for a contingent fee or a commission, or receives a contingent fee or commission from an audit client.

(6) Partner rotation. (i) Except as provided in paragraph (c)(6)(ii) of this section, an accountant is not independent of an audit client when:

(A) Any audit partner as defined in paragraph (f)(7)(ii) of this section performs:

(1) The services of a lead partner, as defined in paragraph (f)(7)(ii)(A) of this section, or concurring partner, as defined in paragraph (f)(7)(ii)(B) of this section, for more than five consecutive years; or

15

(2) One or more of the services defined in paragraphs (f)(7)(ii)(C) and (D) of this section for more than seven consecutive years;

(B) Any audit partner:

(1) Within the five consecutive year period following the performance of services for the maximum period permitted under paragraph (c)(6)(i)(A)(1) of this section, performs for that audit client the services of a lead partner, as defined in paragraph (f)(7)(ii)(A) of this section, or concurring partner, as defined in paragraph (f)(7)(ii)(B) of this section, or a combination of those services, or

(2) Within the two consecutive year period following the performance of services for the maximum period permitted under paragraph (c)(6)(i)(A)(2) of this section, performs one or more of the services defined in paragraph (f)(7)(ii) of this section.

(ii) Any accounting firm with less than five audit clients that are issuers (as defined in section 10A(f) of the Securities Exchange Act of 1934 (15 U.S.C. 78j-1(f))) and less than ten partners shall be exempt from paragraph (c)(6)(i) of this section provided the Public Company Accounting Oversight Board conducts a review at least once every three years of each of the audit client engagements that would result in a lack of auditor independence under this paragraph.

(iii) For purposes of paragraph (c)(6)(i) of this section, an audit client that is an investment company registered under section 8 of the Investment Company Act of 1940 (15 U.S.C. 80a-8), does not include an affiliate of the audit client that is an entity in the same investment company complex, as defined in paragraph (f)(14) of this section, except for another registered investment company in the same investment company complex. For purposes of calculating consecutive years of service under paragraph (c)(6)(i) of this section with respect to investment companies in an investment company complex, audits of registered investment companies with different fiscal year-ends that are performed in a continuous 12-month period count as a single consecutive year.

(7) Audit committee administration of the engagement. An accountant is not independent of an issuer (as defined in section 10A(f) of the Securities Exchange Act of 1934 (15 U.S.C. 78j-1(f))), other than an issuer that is an Asset-Backed Issuer as defined in §229.1101 of this chapter, or an investment company registered under section 8 of the Investment Company Act of 1940 (15 U.S.C. 80a-8), other than a unit investment trust as defined by section 4(2) of the Investment Company Act of 1940 (15 U.S.C. 80a-4(2)), unless:

(i) In accordance with Section 10A(i) of the Securities Exchange Act of 1934 (15 U.S.C. 78j-1(i)) either:

(A) Before the accountant is engaged by the issuer or its subsidiaries, or the registered investment company or its subsidiaries, to render audit or non-audit services, the engagement is approved by the issuer's or registered investment company's audit committee; or

(B) The engagement to render the service is entered into pursuant to pre-approval policies and procedures established by the audit committee of the issuer or registered investment company, provided the policies and procedures are detailed as to the particular service and the audit committee is informed of each service and such policies and procedures do not include delegation of the audit committees responsibilities under the Securities Exchange Act of 1934 to management; or

(C) With respect to the provision of services other than audit, review or attest services the pre-approval requirement is waived if:

(1) The aggregate amount of all such services provided constitutes no more than five percent of the total amount of revenues paid by the audit client to its accountant during the fiscal year in which the services are provided;

(2) Such services were not recognized by the issuer or registered investment company at the time of the engagement to be non-audit services; and

(3) Such services are promptly brought to the attention of the audit committee of the issuer or registered investment company and approved prior to the completion of the audit by the audit committee or by one or more members of the audit committee who are members of the board of directors to whom authority to grant such approvals has been delegated by the audit committee.

(ii) A registered investment company's audit committee also must pre-approve its accountant's engagements for non-audit services with the registered investment company's investment adviser (not including a sub-adviser whose role is primarily portfolio management and is sub-contracted or overseen by another investment adviser) and any entity controlling, controlled by, or under common control with the investment adviser that provides ongoing services to the registered investment company in accordance with paragraph (c)(7)(i) of this section, if the engagement relates directly to the operations and financial reporting of the registered investment company, except that with respect to the waiver of the pre-approval requirement under paragraph (c)(7)(i)(C) of this section, the aggregate amount of all services provided constitutes no more than five percent of the total amount of revenues paid to the registered investment company's accountant by the registered investment company, its investment adviser and any entity controlling, controlled by, or under common control with the investment adviser that provides ongoing services to the registered investment company during the fiscal year in which the services are provided that would have to be pre-approved by the registered investment company's audit committee pursuant to this section.

(8) Compensation. An accountant is not independent of an audit client if, at any point during the audit and professional engagement period, any audit partner earns or receives compensation based on the audit partner procuring engagements with that audit client to provide any products or services other than audit, review or attest services. Any accounting firm with fewer than ten partners and fewer than five audit clients that are issuers (as defined in section 10A(f) of the Securities Exchange Act of 1934 (15 U.S.C. 78j-1(f))) shall be exempt from the requirement stated in the previous sentence.

(d) Quality controls. An accounting firm's independence will not be impaired solely because a covered person in the firm is not independent of an audit client provided:

(1) The covered person did not know of the circumstances giving rise to the lack of independence;

(2) The covered person's lack of independence was corrected as promptly as possible under the relevant circumstances after the covered person or accounting firm became aware of it; and

(3) The accounting firm has a quality control system in place that provides reasonable assurance, taking into account the size and nature of the accounting firm's practice, that the accounting firm and its employees do not lack independence, and that covers at least all employees and associated entities of the accounting firm participating in the engagement, including employees and associated entities located outside of the United States.

(4) For an accounting firm that annually provides audit, review, or attest services to more than 500 companies with a class of securities registered with the Commission under section 12 of the Securities Exchange Act of 1934 (15 U.S.C. 78l), a quality control system will not provide such reasonable assurance unless it has at least the following features:

(i) Written independence policies and procedures;

(ii) With respect to partners and managerial employees, an automated system to identify their investments in securities that might impair the accountant's independence;

(iii) With respect to all professionals, a system that provides timely information about entities from which the accountant is required to maintain independence;

(iv) An annual or on-going firm-wide training program about auditor independence;

(v) An annual internal inspection and testing program to monitor adherence to independence requirements;

(vi) Notification to all accounting firm members, officers, directors, and employees of the name and title of the member of senior management responsible for compliance with auditor independence requirements;

(vii) Written policies and procedures requiring all partners and covered persons to report promptly to the accounting firm when they are engaged in employment negotiations with an audit client, and requiring the firm to remove immediately any such professional from that audit client's engagement and to review promptly all work the professional performed related to that audit client's engagement; and

(viii) A disciplinary mechanism to ensure compliance with this section.

(e)(1) Transition and grandfathering. Provided the following relationships did not impair the accountant's independence under pre-existing requirements of the Commission, the Independence Standards, Board, or the accounting profession in the United States, the existence of the relationship on May 6, 2003 will not be deemed to impair an accountant's independence:

(i) Employment relationships that commenced at the issuer prior to May 6, 2003 as described in paragraph (c)(2)(iii)(B) of this section.

(ii) Compensation earned or received, as described in paragraph (c)(8) of this section during the fiscal year of the accounting firm that includes the effective date of this section.

(iii) Until May 6, 2004, the provision of services described in paragraph (c)(4) of this section provided those services are pursuant to contracts in existence on May 6, 2003.

(iv) The provision of services by the accountant under contracts in existence on May 6, 2003 that have not been pre-approved by the audit committee as described in paragraph (c)(7) of this section.

(v) Until the first day of the issuer's fiscal year beginning after May 6, 2003 by a "lead" partner and other audit partner (other than the "concurring" partner) providing services in excess of those permitted under paragraph (c)(6) of this section. An accountant's independence will not be deemed to be impaired until the first day of the issuer's fiscal year beginning after May 6, 2004 by a "concurring" partner providing services in excess of those permitted under paragraph (c)(6) of this section. For the purposes of calculating periods of service under paragraph (c)(6) of this section:

(A) For the "lead" and "concurring" partner, the period of service includes time served as the "lead" or "concurring" partner prior to May 6, 2003; and

(B) For audit partners other than the "lead" partner or "concurring" partner, and for audit partners in foreign firms, the period of service does not include time served on the audit engagement team prior to the first day of issuer's fiscal year beginning on or after May 6, 2003.

(2) Settling financial arrangements with former professionals. To the extent not required by pre-existing requirements of the Commission, the Independence Standards Board, or the accounting profession in the United States, the requirement in paragraph (c)(2)(iii) of this section to settle financial arrangements with former professionals applies to situations that arise after the effective date of this section.

(f) Definitions of terms. For purposes of this section:

(1) Accountant, as used in paragraphs (b) through (e) of this section, means a registered public accounting firm, certified public accountant or public accountant performing services in connection with an engagement for which independence is required. References to the accountant include any accounting firm with which the certified public accountant or public accountant is affiliated.

(2) Accounting firm means an organization (whether it is a sole proprietorship, incorporated association, partnership, corporation, limited liability company, limited liability partnership, or other legal entity) that is engaged in the practice of public accounting and furnishes reports or other documents filed with the Commission or otherwise prepared under the securities laws, and all of the organization's departments, divisions, parents, subsidiaries, and associated entities, including those located outside of the United States. Accounting firm also includes the organization's pension, retirement, investment, or similar plans.

(3)(i) Accounting role means a role in which a person is in a position to or does exercise more than minimal influence over the contents of the accounting records or anyone who prepares them.

(ii) Financial reporting oversight role means a role in which a person is in a position to or does exercise influence over the contents of the financial statements or anyone who prepares them, such as when the person is a member of the board of directors or similar management or governing body, chief executive officer, president, chief financial officer, chief operating officer, general counsel, chief accounting officer, controller, director of internal audit, director of financial reporting, treasurer, or any equivalent position.

(4) Affiliate of the audit client means:

(i) An entity that has control over the audit client, or over which the audit client has control, or which is under common control with the audit client, including the audit client's parents and subsidiaries;

(ii) An entity over which the audit client has significant influence, unless the entity is not material to the audit client;

(iii) An entity that has significant influence over the audit client, unless the audit client is not material to the entity; and

(iv) Each entity in the investment company complex when the audit client is an entity that is part of an investment company complex.

(5) Audit and professional engagement period includes both:

(i) The period covered by any financial statements being audited or reviewed (the "audit period"); and

(ii) The period of the engagement to audit or review the audit client's financial statements or to prepare a report filed with the Commission (the "professional engagement period"):

(A) The professional engagement period begins when the accountant either signs an initial engagement letter (or other agreement to review or audit a client's financial statements) or begins audit, review, or attest procedures, whichever is earlier; and

(B) The professional engagement period ends when the audit client or the accountant notifies the Commission that the client is no longer that accountant's audit client.

(iii) For audits of the financial statements of foreign private issuers, the "audit and professional engagement period" does not include periods ended prior to the first day of the last fiscal year before the foreign private issuer first filed, or was required to file, a registration statement or report with the Commission, provided there has been full compliance with home country independence standards in all prior periods covered by any registration statement or report filed with the Commission.

(6) Audit client means the entity whose financial statements or other information is being audited, reviewed, or attested and any affiliates of the audit client, other than, for purposes of paragraph (c)(1)(i) of this section, entities that are affiliates of the audit client only by virtue of paragraph (f)(4)(ii) or (f)(4)(iii) of this section.

(7)(i) Audit engagement team means all partners, principals, shareholders and professional employees participating in an audit, review, or attestation engagement of an audit client, including audit partners and all persons who consult with others on the audit engagement team during the audit, review, or attestation engagement regarding technical or industry-specific issues, transactions, or events.

(ii) Audit partner means a partner or persons in an equivalent position, other than a partner who consults with others on the audit engagement team during the audit, review, or attestation engagement regarding technical or industry-specific issues, transactions, or events, who is a member of the audit engagement team who has responsibility for decision-making on significant auditing, accounting, and reporting matters that affect the financial statements, or who maintains regular contact with management and the audit committee and includes the following:

(A) The lead or coordinating audit partner having primary responsibility for the audit or review (the "lead partner");

(B) The partner performing a second level of review to provide additional assurance that the financial statements subject to the audit or review are in conformity with generally accepted accounting principles and the audit or review and any associated report are in accordance with generally accepted auditing standards and rules promulgated by the Commission or the Public Company Accounting Oversight Board (the "concurring or reviewing partner");

(C) Other audit engagement team partners who provide more than ten hours of audit, review, or attest services in connection with the annual or interim consolidated financial statements of the issuer or an investment company registered under section 8 of the Investment Company Act of 1940 (15 U.S.C. 80a-8); and

(D) Other audit engagement team partners who serve as the "lead partner" in connection with any audit or review related to the annual or interim financial statements of a subsidiary of the issuer whose assets or revenues constitute 20% or more of the assets or revenues of the issuer's respective consolidated assets or revenues.

(8) Chain of command means all persons who:

(i) Supervise or have direct management responsibility for the audit, including at all successively senior levels through the accounting firm's chief executive;

(ii) Evaluate the performance or recommend the compensation of the audit engagement partner; or

(iii) Provide quality control or other oversight of the audit.

(9) Close family members means a person's spouse, spousal equivalent, parent, dependent, nondependent child, and sibling.

(10) Contingent fee means, except as stated in the next sentence, any fee established for the sale of a product or the performance of any service pursuant to an arrangement in which no fee will be charged unless a specified finding or result is attained, or in which the amount of the fee is otherwise dependent upon the finding or result of such product or service. Solely for the purposes of this section, a fee is not a "contingent fee" if it is fixed by courts or other public authorities, or, in tax matters, if determined based on the results of judicial proceedings or the findings of governmental agencies. Fees may vary depending, for example, on the complexity of services rendered.

(11) Covered persons in the firm means the following partners, principals, shareholders, and employees of an accounting firm:

(i) The "audit engagement team";

(ii) The "chain of command";

(iii) Any other partner, principal, shareholder, or managerial employee of the accounting firm who has provided ten or more hours of non-audit services to the audit client for the period beginning on the date such services are provided and ending on the date the accounting firm signs the report on the financial statements for the fiscal year during which those services are provided, or who expects to provide ten or more hours of non-audit services to the audit client on a recurring basis; and

(iv) Any other partner, principal, or shareholder from an "office" of the accounting firm in which the lead audit engagement partner primarily practices in connection with the audit.

(12) Group means two or more persons who act together for the purposes of acquiring, holding, voting, or disposing of securities of a registrant.

(13) Immediate family members means a person's spouse, spousal equivalent, and dependents.

(14) Investment company complex. (i) "Investment company complex" includes:

(A) An investment company and its investment adviser or sponsor;

(B) Any entity controlled by or controlling an investment adviser or sponsor in paragraph (f)(14)(i)(A) of this section, or any entity under common control with an investment adviser or sponsor in paragraph (f)(14)(i)(A) of this section if the entity:

(1) Is an investment adviser or sponsor; or

(2) Is engaged in the business of providing administrative, custodian, underwriting, or transfer agent services to any investment company, investment adviser, or sponsor; and

(C) Any investment company or entity that would be an investment company but for the exclusions provided by section 3(c) of the Investment Company Act of 1940 (15 U.S.C. 80a-3(c)) that has an investment adviser or sponsor included in this definition by either paragraph (f)(14)(i)(A) or (f)(14)(i)(B) of this section.

(ii) An investment adviser, for purposes of this definition, does not include a sub-adviser whose role is primarily portfolio management and is subcontracted with or overseen by another investment adviser.

(iii) Sponsor, for purposes of this definition, is an entity that establishes a unit investment trust.

(15) Office means a distinct sub-group within an accounting firm, whether distinguished along geographic or practice lines.

(16) Rabbi trust means an irrevocable trust whose assets are not accessible to the accounting firm until all benefit obligations have been met, but are subject to the claims of creditors in bankruptcy or insolvency.

(17) Audit committee means a committee (or equivalent body) as defined in section 3(a)(58) of the Securities Exchange Act of 1934 (15 U.S.C. 78c(a)(58)).

[37 FR 14594, July 21, 1972, as amended at 48 FR 9521, Mar. 7, 1983; 65 FR 76082, Dec. 5, 2000; 68 FR 6044, Feb. 5, 2003; 70 FR 1593, Jan. 7, 2005]

§210.2-02 Accountants' reports and attestation reports.
(a) Technical requirements for accountants' reports. The accountant's report:

(1) Shall be dated;

(2) Shall be signed manually;

(3) Shall indicate the city and State where issued; and

(4) Shall identify without detailed enumeration the financial statements covered by the report.

(b) Representations as to the audit included in accountants' reports. The accountant's report:

(1) Shall state whether the audit was made in accordance with generally accepted auditing standards; and

(2) Shall designate any auditing procedures deemed necessary by the accountant under the circumstances of the particular case, which have been omitted, and the reasons for their omission. Nothing in this rule shall be construed to imply authority for the omission of any procedure which independent accountants would ordinarily employ in the course of an audit made for the purpose of expressing the opinions required by paragraph (c) of this section.

(c) Opinions to be expressed in accountants' reports. The accountant's report shall state clearly:

(1) The opinion of the accountant in respect of the financial statements covered by the report and the accounting principles and practices reflected therein; and

(2) the opinion of the accountant as to the consistency of the application of the accounting principles, or as to any changes in such principles which have a material effect on the financial statements.

(d) Exceptions identified in accountants' reports. Any matters to which the accountant takes exception shall be clearly identified, the exception thereto specifically and clearly stated, and, to the extent practicable, the effect of each such exception on the related financial statements given. (See section 101 of the Codification of Financial Reporting Policies.)

(e) Paragraph (e) of this section applies only to registrants that are providing financial statements in a filing for a period with respect to which Arthur Andersen LLP or a foreign affiliate of Arthur Andersen LLP ("Andersen") issued an accountants' report. Notwithstanding any other Commission rule or regulation, a registrant that cannot obtain an accountants' report that meets the technical requirements of paragraph (a) of this section after reasonable efforts may include in the document a copy of the latest signed and dated accountants' report issued by Andersen for such period in satisfaction of that requirement, if prominent disclosure that the report is a copy of the previously issued Andersen accountants' report and that the report has not been reissued by Andersen is set forth on such copy.

(f) Attestation report on internal control over financial reporting. (1) Every registered public accounting firm that issues or prepares an accountant's report for a registrant, other than a registrant that is neither an accelerated filer nor a large accelerated filer (as defined in §240.12b-2 of this chapter), or is an emerging growth company, as defined in Rule 405 of the Securities Act (§230.405 of this chapter) or Rule 12b-2 of the Exchange Act (§240.12b-2 of this chapter), or an investment company registered under Section 8 of the Investment Company Act of 1940

(15 U.S.C. 80a-8), that is included in an annual report required by section 13(a) or 15(d) of the Securities Exchange Act of 1934 (15 U.S.C. 78a et seq.) containing an assessment by management of the effectiveness of the registrant's internal control over financial reporting must include an attestation report on internal control over financial reporting.

(2) If an attestation report on internal control over financial reporting is included in an annual report required by section 13(a) or 15(d) of the Securities Exchange Act of 1934 (15 U.S.C. 78a et seq.), it shall clearly state the opinion of the accountant, either unqualified or adverse, as to whether the registrant maintained, in all material respects, effective internal control over financial reporting, except in the rare circumstance of a scope limitation that cannot be overcome by the registrant or the registered public accounting firm which would result in the accounting firm disclaiming an opinion. The attestation report on internal control over financial reporting shall be dated, signed manually, identify the period covered by the report and indicate that the accountant has audited the effectiveness of internal control over financial reporting. The attestation report on internal control over financial reporting may be separate from the accountant's report.

(g) Attestation report on assessment of compliance with servicing criteria for asset-backed securities. The attestation report on assessment of compliance with servicing criteria for asset-backed securities, as required by §240.13a-18(c) or §240.15d-18(c) of this chapter, shall be dated, signed manually, identify the period covered by the report and clearly state the opinion of the registered public accounting firm as to whether the asserting party's assessment of compliance with the servicing criteria is fairly stated in all material respects, or must include an opinion to the effect that an overall opinion cannot be expressed. If an overall opinion cannot be expressed, explain why.

[37 FR 14594, July 21, 1972, as amended at 41 FR 35479, Aug. 23, 1976; 45 FR 63668, Sept. 25, 1980; 50 FR 25215, June 18, 1985; 67 FR 13533, Mar. 22, 2002; 68 FR 36660, June 18, 2003; 70 FR 1593, Jan. 7, 2005; 72 FR 35321, June 27, 2007; 75 FR 57387, Sept. 21, 2010; 82 FR 17551, Apr. 12, 2017]

§210.2-03 Examination of financial statements by foreign government auditors.
Notwithstanding any requirements as to examination by independent accountants, the financial statements of any foreign governmental agency may be examined by the regular and customary auditing staff of the respective government if public financial statements of such governmental agency are customarily examined by such auditing staff.

§210.2-04 Examination of financial statements of persons other than the registrant.
If a registrant is required to file financial statements of any other person, such statements need not be examined if examination of such statements would not be required if such person were itself a registrant.

§210.2-05 Examination of financial statements by more than one accountant.

If, with respect to the examination of the financial statements, part of the examination is made by an independent accountant other than the principal accountant and the principal accountant elects to place reliance on the work of the other accountant and makes reference to that effect in his report, the separate report of the other accountant shall be filed. However, notwithstanding the provisions of this section, reports of other accountants which may otherwise be required in filings need not be presented in annual reports to security holders furnished pursuant to the proxy and information statement rules under the Securities Exchange Act of 1934 [§§240.14a-3 and 240.14c-3].

[46 FR 40872, Aug. 13, 1981]

§210.2-06 Retention of audit and review records.

(a) For a period of seven years after an accountant concludes an audit or review of an issuer's financial statements to which section 10A(a) of the Securities Exchange Act of 1934 (15 U.S.C. 78j-1(a)) applies, or of the financial statements of any investment company registered under section 8 of the Investment Company Act of 1940 (15 U.S.C. 80a-8), the accountant shall retain records relevant to the audit or review, including workpapers and other documents that form the basis of the audit or review, and memoranda, correspondence, communications, other documents, and records (including electronic records), which:

(1) Are created, sent or received in connection with the audit or review, and

(2) Contain conclusions, opinions, analyses, or financial data related to the audit or review.

(b) For the purposes of paragraph (a) of this section, workpapers means documentation of auditing or review procedures applied, evidence obtained, and conclusions reached by the accountant in the audit or review engagement, as required by standards established or adopted by the Commission or by the Public Company Accounting Oversight Board.

(c) Memoranda, correspondence, communications, other documents, and records (including electronic records) described in paragraph (a) of this section shall be retained whether they support the auditor's final conclusions regarding the audit or review, or contain information or data, relating to a significant matter, that is inconsistent with the auditor's final conclusions regarding that matter or the audit or review. Significance of a matter shall be determined based on an objective analysis of the facts and circumstances. Such documents and records include, but are not limited to, those documenting a consultation on or resolution of differences in professional judgment.

(d) For the purposes of paragraph (a) of this section, the term issuer means an issuer as defined in section 10A(f) of the Securities Exchange Act of 1934 (15 U.S.C. 78j-1(f)).

[68 FR 4872, Jan. 30, 2003]

§210.2-07 Communication with audit committees.

(a) Each registered public accounting firm that performs for an audit client that is an issuer (as defined in section 10A(f) of the Securities Exchange Act of 1934 (15 U.S.C. 78j-1(f))), other than an issuer that is an Asset-Backed Issuer as defined in §229.1101 of this chapter, or an investment company registered under section 8 of the Investment Company Act of 1940 (15 U.S.C. 80a-8), other than a unit investment trust as defined by section 4(2) of the Investment Company Act of 1940 (15 U.S.C. 80a-4(2)), any audit required under the securities laws shall report, prior to the filing of such audit report with the Commission (or in the case of a registered investment company, annually, and if the annual communication is not within 90 days prior to the filing, provide an update, in the 90 day period prior to the filing, of any changes to the previously reported information), to the audit committee of the issuer or registered investment company:

(1) All critical accounting policies and practices to be used;

(2) All alternative treatments within Generally Accepted Accounting Principles for policies and practices related to material items that have been discussed with management of the issuer or registered investment company, including:

(i) Ramifications of the use of such alternative disclosures and treatments; and

(ii) The treatment preferred by the registered public accounting firm;

(3) Other material written communications between the registered public accounting firm and the management of the issuer or registered investment company, such as any management letter or schedule of unadjusted differences;

(4) If the audit client is an investment company, all non-audit services provided to any entity in an investment company complex, as defined in §210.2-01 (f)(14), that were not pre-approved by the registered investment company's audit committee pursuant to §210.2-01 (c)(7).

(b) [Reserved]

[68 FR 6048, Feb. 5, 2003, as amended at 70 FR 1593, Jan. 7, 2005]

General Instructions as to Financial Statements

Source: Sections 210.3-01 through 210.3-16 appear at 45 FR 63687, Sept. 25, 1980, unless otherwise noted.

Note: These instructions specify the balance sheets and statements of income and cash flows to be included in disclosure documents prepared in accordance with Regulation S-X. Other portions of Regulation S-X govern the examination, form and content of such financial statements, including the basis of consolidation and the schedules to be filed. The financial statements described below shall be audited unless otherwise indicated.

For filings under the Securities Act of 1933, attention is directed to §230.411(b) regarding incorporation by reference to financial statements and to section 10(a)(3) of the Act regarding information required in the prospectus.

For filings under the Securities Exchange Act of 1934, attention is directed to §240.12b-23 regarding incorporation by reference and §240.12b-36 regarding use of financial statements filed under other acts.

[45 FR 63687, Sept. 25, 1980, as amended at 57 FR 45292, Oct. 1, 1992]

§210.3-01 Consolidated balance sheets.

(a) There shall be filed, for the registrant and its subsidiaries consolidated, audited balance sheets as of the end of each of the two most recent fiscal years. If the registrant has been in existence for less than one fiscal year, there shall be filed an audited balance sheet as of a date within 135 days of the date of filing the registration statement.

(b) If the filing, other than a filing on Form 10-K or Form 10, is made within 45 days after the end of the registrant's fiscal year and audited financial statements for the most recent fiscal year are not available, the balance sheets may be as of the end of the two preceding fiscal years and the filing shall include an additional balance sheet as of an interim date at least as current as the end of the registrant's third fiscal quarter of the most recently completed fiscal year.

(c) The instruction in paragraph (b) of this section is also applicable to filings, other than on Form 10-K or Form 10, made after 45 days but within the number of days of the end of the registrant's fiscal year specified in paragraph (i) of this section: Provided, that the following conditions are met:

(1) The registrant files annual, quarterly and other reports pursuant to section 13 or 15(d) of the Securities Exchange Act of 1934 and all reports due have been filed;

(2) For the most recent fiscal year for which audited financial statements are not yet available the registrant reasonably and in good faith expects to report income attributable to the registrant, after taxes but before extraordinary items and cumulative effect of a change in accounting principle; and

(3) For at least one of the two fiscal years immediately preceding the most recent fiscal year the registrant reported income attributable to the registrant, after taxes but before extraordinary items and cumulative effect of a change in accounting principle.

(d) For filings made after 45 days but within the number of days of the end of the registrant's fiscal year specified in paragraph (i) of this section where the conditions set forth in paragraph (c) of this section are not met, the filing must include the audited balance sheets required by paragraph (a) of this section.

(e) For filings made after the number of days specified in paragraph (i)(2) of this section, the filing shall also include a balance sheet as of an interim date within the following number of days of the date of filing:

(1) 130 days for large accelerated filers and accelerated filers (as defined in §240.12b-2 of this chapter); and

(2) 135 days for all other registrants.

(f) Any interim balance sheet provided in accordance with the requirements of this section may be unaudited and need not be presented in greater detail than is required by §210.10-01. Notwithstanding the requirements of this section, the most recent interim balance sheet included in a filing shall be at least as current as the most recent balance sheet filed with the Commission on Form 10-Q.

(g) For filings by registered management investment companies, the requirements of §210.3-18 shall apply in lieu of the requirements of this section.

(h) Any foreign private issuer, other than a registered management investment company or an employee plan, may file the financial statements required by Item 8.A of Form 20-F (§249.220 of this chapter) in lieu of the financial statements specified in this rule.

(i)(1) For purposes of paragraphs (c) and (d) of this section, the number of days shall be:

(i) 60 days (75 days for fiscal years ending before December 15, 2006) for large accelerated filers (as defined in §240.12b-2 of this chapter);

(ii) 75 days for accelerated filers (as defined in §240.12b-2 of this chapter); and

(iii) 90 days for all other registrants.

(2) For purposes of paragraph (e) of this section, the number of days shall be:

(i) 129 days subsequent to the end of the registrant's most recent fiscal year for large accelerated filers and accelerated filers (as defined in §240.12b-2 of this chapter); and

(ii) 134 days subsequent to the end of the registrant's most recent fiscal year for all other registrants.

[45 FR 63687, Sept. 25, 1980, as amended at 46 FR 12491, Feb. 17, 1981; 46 FR 36124, July 14, 1981; 50 FR 49531, Dec. 3, 1985; 56 FR 30053, July 1, 1991; 64 FR 53908, Oct. 5, 1999; 67 FR 58503, Sept. 16, 2002; 68 FR 17880, Apr. 14, 2003; 69 FR 68235, Nov. 23, 2004; 70 FR 76640, Dec. 27, 2005; 73 FR 952, Jan. 4, 2008; 74 FR 18614, Apr. 23, 2009]

§210.3-02 Consolidated statements of income and changes in financial positions.

(a) There shall be filed, for the registrant and its subsidiaries consolidated and for its predecessors, audited statements of income and cash flows for each of the three fiscal years preceding the date of the most recent audited balance sheet being filed or such shorter period as the registrant (including predecessors) has been in existence. A registrant that is an emerging growth company, as defined in Rule 405 of the Securities Act (§230.405 of this chapter) or Rule 12b-2 of the Exchange Act (§240.12b-2 of this chapter), may, in a Securities Act registration statement for the initial public offering of the emerging growth company's equity securities, provide audited statements of income and cash flows for each of the two fiscal years preceding the date of the most recent audited balance sheet (or such shorter period as the registrant has been in existence).

(b) In addition, for any interim period between the latest audited balance sheet and the date of the most recent interim balance sheet being filed, and for the corresponding period of the preceding fiscal year, statements of income and cash flows shall be provided. Such interim financial statements may be unaudited and need not be presented in greater detail than is required by §210.10-01.

(c) For filings by registered management investment companies, the requirements of §210.3-18 shall apply in lieu of the requirements of this section.

(d) Any foreign private issuer, other than a registered management investment company or an employee plan, may file the financial statements required by Item 8.A of Form 20-F (§249.220 of this chapter) in lieu of the financial statements specified in this rule.

[45 FR 63687, Sept. 25, 1980, as amended at 46 FR 12491, Feb. 17, 1981; 46 FR 36125, July 14, 1981; 50 FR 49531, Dec. 3, 1985; 56 FR 30053, July 1, 1991; 57 FR 45292, Oct. 1, 1992; 64 FR 53908, Oct. 5, 1999; 82 FR 17551, Apr. 12, 2017]

§210.3-03 Instructions to income statement requirements.

(a) The statements required shall be prepared in compliance with the applicable requirements of this regulation.

(b) If the registrant is engaged primarily (1) in the generation, transmission or distribution of electricity, the manufacture, mixing, transmission or distribution of gas, the supplying or distribution of water, or the furnishing of telephone or telegraph service; or (2) in holding securities of companies engaged in such businesses, it may at its option include statements of income and cash flows (which may be unaudited) for the twelve-month period ending on the date of the most recent balance sheet being filed, in lieu of the statements of income and cash flows for the interim periods specified.

(c) If a period or periods reported on include operations of a business prior to the date of acquisition, or for other reasons differ from reports previously issued for any period, the statements shall be reconciled as to sales or revenues and net income in the statement or in a note thereto with the amounts previously reported: Provided, however, That such reconciliations need not be made (1) if they have been made in filings with the Commission in prior years or (2) the financial statements which are being retroactively adjusted have not previously been filed with the Commission or otherwise made public.

(d) Any unaudited interim financial statements furnished shall reflect all adjustments which are, in the opinion of management, necessary to a fair statement of the results for the interim periods presented. A statement to that effect shall be included. Such adjustments shall include, for example, appropriate estimated provisions for bonus and profit sharing arrangements normally determined or settled at year-end. If all such adjustments are of a normal recurring nature, a statement to that effect shall be made; otherwise, there shall be furnished information describing in appropriate detail the nature and amount of any adjustments other than normal recurring adjustments entering into the determination of the results shown.

(e) Disclosures regarding segments required by generally accepted accounting principles shall be provided for each year for which an audited statement of income is provided. To the extent that the segment information presented pursuant to this instruction complies with the provisions of Item 101 of Regulation S-K, the disclosures may be combined by cross referencing to or from the financial statements.

[45 FR 63687, Sept. 25, 1980. Redesignated at 47 FR 29836, July 9, 1982, and amended at 50 FR 25215, June 18, 1985; 50 FR 49532, Dec. 3, 1985; 57 FR 45292, Oct. 1, 1992; 64 FR 1734, Jan. 12, 1999]

§210.3-04 Changes in stockholders' equity and noncontrolling interests.

An analysis of the changes in each caption of stockholders' equity and noncontrolling interests presented in the balance sheets shall be given in a note or separate statement. This analysis shall be presented in the form of a reconciliation of the beginning balance to the ending balance for each period for which an income statement is required to be filed with all significant reconciling items described by appropriate captions with contributions from and distribution to owners shown separately. Also, state-separately the adjustments to the balance at the beginning of the earliest period presented for items which were retroactively applied to periods prior to that period. With respect to any dividends, state the amount per share and in the aggregate for each class of shares. Provide a separate schedule in the notes to the financial statements that shows the effects of any changes in the registrant's ownership interest in a subsidiary on the equity attributable to the registrant.

[74 FR 18614, Apr. 23, 2009]

§210.3-05 Financial statements of businesses acquired or to be acquired.

(a) Financial statements required. (1) Financial statements prepared and audited in accordance with this regulation should be furnished for the periods specified in paragraph (b) below if any of the following conditions exist:

(i) A business combination has occurred or is probable (for purposes of this section, this encompasses the acquisition of an interest in a business accounted for by the equity method); or

(ii) Consummation of a combination between entities under common control is probable.

(2) For purposes of determining whether the provisions of this rule apply, the determination of whether a business has been acquired should be made in accordance with the guidance set forth in §210.11-01(d).

(3) Acquisitions of a group of related businesses that are probable or that have occurred subsequent to the latest fiscal year-end for which audited financial statements of the registrant have been filed shall be treated under this section as if they are a single business combination. The required financial statements of related businesses may be presented on a combined basis for any periods they are under common control or management. For purposes of this section, businesses shall be deemed to be related if:

(i) They are under common control or management;

(ii) The acquisition of one business is conditional on the acquisition of each other business; or

(iii) Each acquisition is conditioned on a single common event.

(4) This rule shall not apply to a business which is totally held by the registrant prior to consummation of the transaction.

(b) Periods to be presented. (1) If securities are being registered to be offered to the security holders of the business to be acquired, the financial statements specified in §§210.3-01 and 210.3-02 shall be furnished for the business to be acquired, except as provided otherwise for filings on Form N-14, S-4 or F-4 (§239.23, §239.25 or §239.34 of this chapter). The financial statements covering fiscal years shall be audited except as provided in Item 14 of Schedule 14A (§240.14a-101 of this chapter) with respect to certain proxy statements or in registration statements filed on Forms N-14, S-4 or F-4 (§239.23, §239.25 or §239.34 of this chapter).

(2) In all cases not specified in paragraph (b)(1) of this section, financial statements of the business acquired or to be acquired shall be filed for the periods specified in this paragraph (b)(2) or such shorter period as the business has been in existence. The periods for which such financial statements are to be filed shall be determined using the conditions specified in the definition of significant subsidiary in §210.1-02(w) as follows:

(i) If none of the conditions exceeds 20 percent, financial statements are not required. However, if the aggregate impact of the individually insignificant businesses acquired since the date of the most recent audited balance sheet filed for the registrant exceeds 50%, financial statements covering at least the substantial majority of the businesses acquired shall be furnished. Such financial statements shall be for at least the most recent fiscal year and any interim periods specified in §§210.3-01 and 210.3-02.

(ii) If any of the conditions exceeds 20 percent, but none exceed 40 percent, financial statements shall be furnished for at least the most recent fiscal year and any interim periods specified in §§210.3-01 and 210.3-02.

(iii) If any of the conditions exceeds 40 percent, but none exceed 50 percent, financial statements shall be furnished for at least the two most recent fiscal years and any interim periods specified in §§210.3-01 and 210.3-02.

(iv) If any of the conditions exceed 50 percent, the full financial statements specified in §§210.3-01 and 210.3-02 shall be furnished. However, financial statements for the earliest of the three fiscal years required may be omitted if net revenues reported by the acquired business in its most recent fiscal year are less than $50 million.

(3) The determination shall be made by comparing the most recent annual financial statements of each such business, or group of related businesses on a combined basis, to the registrant's most recent annual consolidated financial statements filed at or prior to the date of acquisition. However, if the registrant made a significant acquisition subsequent to the latest fiscal year-end and filed a report on Form 8-K (§249.308 of this chapter) which included audited financial statements of such acquired business for the periods required by this section and the pro forma financial information required by §210.11, such determination may be made by using pro forma amounts for the latest fiscal year in the report on Form 8-K (§249.308 of this chapter) rather than by using the historical amounts of the registrant. The tests may not be made by "annualizing" data.

(4) Financial statements required for the periods specified in paragraph (b)(2) of this section may be omitted to the extent specified as follows:

(i) Registration statements not subject to the provisions of §230.419 of this chapter (Regulation C) and proxy statements need not include separate financial statements of the acquired or to be acquired business if it does not exceed any of the conditions of significance in the definition of significant subsidiary in §210.1-02 at the 50 percent level, and either:

(A) The consummation of the acquisition has not yet occurred; or

(B) The date of the final prospectus or prospectus supplement relating to an offering as filed with the Commission pursuant to §230.424(b) of this chapter, or mailing date in the case of a proxy statement, is no more than 74 days after consummation of the business combination, and the financial statements have not previously been filed by the registrant.

(ii) An issuer, other than a foreign private issuer required to file reports on Form 6-K, that omits from its initial registration statement financial statements of a recently consummated business combination pursuant to paragraph (b)(4)(i) of this section shall furnish those financial statements and any pro forma information specified by Article 11 of this chapter under cover of Form 8-K (§249.308 of this chapter) no later than 75 days after consummation of the acquisition.

(iii) Separate financial statements of the acquired business need not be presented once the operating results of the acquired business have been reflected in the audited consolidated financial statements of the registrant for a complete fiscal year unless such financial statements have not been previously filed or unless the acquired business is of such significance to the registrant that omission of such financial statements would materially impair an investor's ability to understand the historical financial results of the registrant. For example, if, at the date of acquisition, the acquired business met at least one of the conditions in the definition of significant subsidiary in §210.1-02 at the 80 percent level, the income statements of the acquired business should normally continue to be furnished for such periods prior to the purchase as may be necessary when added to the time for which audited income statements after the purchase are filed to cover the equivalent of the period specified in §210.3-02.

(iv) A separate audited balance sheet of the acquired business is not required when the registrant's most recent audited balance sheet required by §210.3-01 is for a date after the date the acquisition was consummated.

(c) Financial statements of foreign business. If the business acquired or to be acquired is a foreign business, financial statements of the business meeting the requirements of Item 17 of Form 20-F (§249.220f of this chapter) will satisfy this section.

[47 FR 29836, July 9, 1982, as amended at 50 FR 49532, Dec. 3, 1985; 51 FR 42056, Nov. 20, 1986; 59 FR 65636, Dec. 20, 1994; 61 FR 54514, Oct. 18, 1996; 73 FR 952, Jan. 4, 2008; 74 FR 18614, Apr. 23, 2009]

§210.3-06   Financial statements covering a period of nine to twelve months.
Except with respect to registered investment companies, the filing of financial statements covering a period of 9 to 12 months shall be deemed to satisfy a requirement for filing financial statements for a period of 1 year where:

(a) The issuer has changed its fiscal year;

(b) The issuer has made a significant business acquisition for which financial statements are required under §210.3-05 of this chapter and the financial statements covering the interim period pertain to the business being acquired; or

(c) The Commission so permits pursuant to §210.3-13 of this chapter.

Where there is a requirement for filing financial statements for a time period exceeding one year but not exceeding three consecutive years (with not more than 12 months included in any period reported upon), the filing of financial statements covering a period of nine to 12 months shall satisfy a filing requirement of financial statements for one year of that time period only if the conditions described in either paragraph (a), (b), or (c) of this section exist and financial statements are filed that cover the full fiscal year or years for all other years in the time period.

[54 FR 10315, Mar. 13, 1989]

§§210.3-07--210.3-08 [Reserved]

§210.3-09 Separate financial statements of subsidiaries not consolidated and 50 percent or less owned persons.

(a) If any of the conditions set forth in §210.1-02(w), substituting 20 percent for 10 percent in the tests used therein to determine a significant subsidiary, are met for a majority-owned subsidiary not consolidated by the registrant or by a subsidiary of the registrant, separate financial statements of such subsidiary shall be filed. Similarly, if either the first or third condition set forth in §210.1-02(w), substituting 20 percent for 10 percent, is met by a 50 percent or less owned person accounted for by the equity method either by the registrant or a subsidiary of the registrant, separate financial statements of such 50 percent or less owned person shall be filed.

(b) Insofar as practicable, the separate financial statements required by this section shall be as of the same dates and for the same periods as the audited consolidated financial statements required by §§210.3-01 and 3-02. However, these separate financial statements are required to be audited only for those fiscal years in which either the first or third condition set forth in §210.1-02(w), substituting 20 percent for 10 percent, is met. For purposes of a filing on Form 10-K (§249.310 of this chapter):

(1) If the registrant is an accelerated filer (as defined in §240.12b-2 of this chapter) but the 50 percent or less owned person is not an accelerated filer, the required financial statements may be filed as an amendment to the report within 90 days, or within six months if the 50 percent or less owned person is a foreign business, after the end of the registrant's fiscal year.

(2) If the fiscal year of any 50 percent or less owned person ends within the registrant's number of filing days before the date of the filing, or if the fiscal year ends after the date of the filing, the required financial statements may be filed as an amendment to the report within the subsidiary's number of filing days, or within six months if the 50 percent or less owned person is a foreign business, after the end of such subsidiary's or person's fiscal year.

(3) The term registrant's number of filing days means:

(i) 60 days (75 days for fiscal years ending before December 15, 2006) if the registrant is a large accelerated filer;

(ii) 75 days if the registrant is an accelerated filer; and

(iii) 90 days for all other registrants.

(4) The term subsidiary's number of filing days means:

(i) 60 days (75 days for fiscal years ending before December 15, 2006) if the 50 percent or less owned person is a large accelerated filer;

(ii) 75 days if the 50 percent or less owned person is an accelerated filer; and

35

(iii) 90 days for all other 50 percent or less owned persons.

(c) Notwithstanding the requirements for separate financial statements in paragraph (a) of this section, where financial statements of two or more majority-owned subsidiaries not consolidated are required, combined or consolidated statements of such subsidiaries may be filed subject to principles of inclusion and exclusion which clearly exhibit the financial position, cash flows and results of operations of the combined or consolidated group. Similarly, where financial statements of two or more 50 percent or less owned persons are required, combined or consolidated statements of such persons may be filed subject to the same principles of inclusion or exclusion referred to above.

(d) If the 50 percent or less owned person is a foreign business, financial statements of the business meeting the requirements of Item 17 of Form 20-F (§249.220f of this chapter) will satisfy this section.

[46 FR 56179, Nov. 16, 1981, as amended at 47 FR 29837, July 9, 1982; 57 FR 45292, Oct. 1, 1992; 59 FR 65636, Dec. 20, 1994; 67 FR 58504, Sept. 16, 2002; 69 FR 68235, Nov. 23, 2004; 70 FR 76640, Dec. 27, 2005]

§210.3-10   Financial statements of guarantors and issuers of guaranteed securities registered or being registered.

(a)(1) General rule. Every issuer of a registered security that is guaranteed and every guarantor of a registered security must file the financial statements required for a registrant by Regulation S-X.

(2) Operation of this rule. Paragraphs (b), (c), (d), (e) and (f) of this section are exceptions to the general rule of paragraph (a)(1) of this section. Only one of these paragraphs can apply to a single issuer or guarantor. Paragraph (g) of this section is a special rule for recently acquired issuers or guarantors that overrides each of these exceptions for a specific issuer or guarantor. Paragraph (h) of this section defines the following terms used in this section: 100% owned, full and unconditional, annual report, quarterly report, no independent assets or operations, minor, finance subsidiary and operating subsidiary. Paragraph (i) of this section states the requirements for preparing the condensed consolidating financial information required by paragraphs (c), (d), (e) and (f) of this section.

Note to paragraph (a)(2). Where paragraphs (b), (c), (d), (e) and (f) of this section specify the filing of financial statements of the parent company, the financial statements of an entity that is not an issuer or guarantor of the registered security cannot be substituted for those of the parent company.

(3) Foreign private issuers. Where any provision of this section requires compliance with §§210.3-01 and 3-02, a foreign private issuer may comply by providing financial statements for the periods specified by Item 8.A of Form 20-F (§249.220f of this chapter).

(b) Finance subsidiary issuer of securities guaranteed by its parent company. When a finance subsidiary issues securities and its parent company guarantees those securities, the registration statement, parent company annual report, or parent company quarterly report need not include financial statements of the issuer if:

(1) The issuer is 100% owned by the parent company guarantor;

(2) The guarantee is full and unconditional;

(3) No other subsidiary of the parent company guarantees the securities; and

(4) The parent company's financial statements are filed for the periods specified by §§210.3-01 and 210.3-02 and include a footnote stating that the issuer is a 100%-owned finance subsidiary of the parent company and the parent company has fully and unconditionally guaranteed the securities. The footnote also must include the narrative disclosures specified in paragraphs (i)(9) and (i)(10) of this section.

Note to paragraph (b): Paragraph (b) is available if a subsidiary issuer satisfies the requirements of this paragraph but for the fact that, instead of the parent company guaranteeing the security, the subsidiary issuer co-issued the security, jointly and severally, with the parent company. In this situation, the narrative information required by paragraph (b)(4) must be modified accordingly.

(c) Operating subsidiary issuer of securities guaranteed by its parent company. When an operating subsidiary issues securities and its parent company guarantees those securities, the registration statement, parent company annual report, or parent company quarterly report need not include financial statements of the issuer if:

(1) The issuer is 100% owned by the parent company guarantor;

(2) The guarantee is full and unconditional;

(3) No other subsidiary of the parent company guarantees the securities; and

(4) The parent company's financial statements are filed for the periods specified by §§210.3-01 and 210.3-02 and include, in a footnote, condensed consolidating financial information for the same periods with a separate column for:

(i) The parent company;

(ii) The subsidiary issuer;

(iii) Any other subsidiaries of the parent company on a combined basis;

(iv) Consolidating adjustments; and

(v) The total consolidated amounts.

Notes to paragraph (c): 1. Instead of the condensed consolidating financial information required by paragraph (c)(4), the parent company's financial statements may include a footnote stating, if true, that the parent company has no independent assets or operations, the guarantee is full and unconditional, and any subsidiaries of the parent company other than the subsidiary issuer are minor. The footnote also must include the narrative disclosures specified in paragraphs (i)(9) and (i)(10) of this section.

2. If the alternative disclosure permitted by Note 1 to this paragraph is not applicable because the parent company has independent assets or operations, the condensed consolidating financial information described in paragraph (c)(4) may omit the column for "any other subsidiaries of the parent company on a combined basis" if those other subsidiaries are minor.

3. Paragraph (c) is available if a subsidiary issuer satisfies the requirements of this paragraph but for the fact that, instead of the parent company guaranteeing the security, the subsidiary issuer co-issued the security, jointly and severally, with the parent company. In this situation, the narrative information required by paragraph (i)(8) of this section must be modified accordingly.

(d) Subsidiary issuer of securities guaranteed by its parent company and one or more other subsidiaries of that parent company. When a subsidiary issues securities and both its parent company and one or more other subsidiaries of that parent company guarantee those securities, the registration statement, parent company annual report, or parent company quarterly report need not include financial statements of the issuer or any subsidiary guarantor if:

(1) The issuer and all subsidiary guarantors are 100% owned by the parent company guarantor;

(2) The guarantees are full and unconditional;

(3) The guarantees are joint and several; and

(4) The parent company's financial statements are filed for the periods specified by §§210.3-01 and 210.3-02 and include, in a footnote, condensed consolidating financial information for the same periods with a separate column for:

(i) The parent company;

(ii) The subsidiary issuer;

(iii) The guarantor subsidiaries of the parent company on a combined basis;

(iv) Any other subsidiaries of the parent company on a combined basis;

(v) Consolidating adjustments; and

(vi) The total consolidated amounts.

Notes to paragraph (d): 1. Paragraph (d) applies in the same manner whether the issuer is a finance subsidiary or an operating subsidiary.

2. The condensed consolidating financial information described in paragraph (d)(4) may omit the column for "any other subsidiaries of the parent company on a combined basis" if those other subsidiaries are minor.

3. Paragraph (d) is available if a subsidiary issuer satisfies the requirements of this paragraph but for the fact that, instead of the parent company guaranteeing the security, the subsidiary issuer co-issued the security, jointly and severally, with the parent company. In this situation, the narrative information required by paragraph (i)(8) of this section must be modified accordingly.

4. If all of the requirements in paragraph (d) are satisfied except that the guarantee of a subsidiary is not joint and several with, as applicable, the parent company's guarantee or the guarantees of the parent company and the other subsidiaries, then each subsidiary guarantor whose guarantee is not joint and several need not include separate financial statements, but the condensed consolidating financial information should include a separate column for each guarantor whose guarantee is not joint and several.

5. Instead of the condensed consolidating financial information required by paragraph (d)(4), the parent company's financial statements may include a footnote stating, if true, that the parent company has no independent assets or operations, the subsidiary issuer is a 100% owned finance subsidiary of the parent company, the parent company has guaranteed the securities, all of the parent company's subsidiaries other than the subsidiary issuer have guaranteed the securities, all of the guarantees are full and unconditional, and all of the guarantees are joint and several. The footnote also must include the narrative disclosures specified in paragraphs (i)(9) and (i)(10) of this section.

(e) Single subsidiary guarantor of securities issued by the parent company of that subsidiary. When a parent company issues securities and one of its subsidiaries guarantees those securities, the registration statement, parent company annual report, or parent company quarterly report need not include financial statements of the subsidiary guarantor if:

(1) The subsidiary guarantor is 100% owned by the parent company issuer;

(2) The guarantee is full and unconditional;

(3) No other subsidiary of that parent guarantees the securities; and

(4) The parent company's financial statements are filed for the periods specified by §§210.3-01 and 210.3-02 and include, in a footnote, condensed consolidating financial information for the same periods with a separate column for:

(i) The parent company;

(ii) The subsidiary guarantor;

(iii) Any other subsidiaries of the parent company on a combined basis;

(iv) Consolidating adjustments; and

(v) The total consolidated amounts.

Notes to paragraph (e): 1. Paragraph (e) applies in the same manner whether the guarantor is a finance subsidiary or an operating subsidiary.

2. Instead of the condensed consolidating financial information required by paragraph (e)(4), the parent company's financial statements may include a footnote stating, if true, that the parent company has no independent assets or operations, the guarantee is full and unconditional, and any subsidiaries of the parent company other than the subsidiary guarantor are minor. The footnote also must include the narrative disclosures specified in paragraphs (i)(9) and (i)(10) of this section.

3. If the alternative disclosure permitted by Note 2 to this paragraph is not applicable because the parent company has independent assets or operations, the condensed consolidating financial information described in paragraph (e)(4) may omit the column for "any other subsidiaries of the parent company on a combined basis" if those other subsidiaries are minor.

4. If, instead of guaranteeing the subject security, a subsidiary co-issues the security jointly and severally with its parent company, this paragraph (e) does not apply. Instead, the appropriate financial information requirement would depend on whether the subsidiary is a finance subsidiary or an operating subsidiary. If the subsidiary is a finance subsidiary, paragraph (b) applies. If the subsidiary is an operating company, paragraph (c) applies.

(f) Multiple subsidiary guarantors of securities issued by the parent company of those subsidiaries. When a parent company issues securities and more than one of its subsidiaries guarantee those securities, the registration statement, parent company annual report, or parent company quarterly report need not include financial statements of the subsidiary guarantors if:

(1) Each of the subsidiary guarantors is 100% owned by the parent company issuer;

(2) The guarantees are full and unconditional;

(3) The guarantees are joint and several; and

(4) The parent company's financial statements are filed for the periods specified by §§210.3-01 and 210.3-02 and include, in a footnote, condensed consolidating financial information for the same periods with a separate column for:

(i) The parent company;

(ii) The subsidiary guarantors on a combined basis;

(iii) Any other subsidiaries of the parent company on a combined basis;

(iv) Consolidating adjustments; and

(v) The total consolidated amounts.

Notes to paragraph (f): 1. Instead of the condensed consolidating financial information required by paragraph (f)(4), the parent company's financial statements may include a footnote stating, if true, that the parent company has no independent assets or operations, the guarantees are full and unconditional and joint and several, and any subsidiaries of the parent company other than the subsidiary guarantors are minor. The footnote also must include the narrative disclosures specified in paragraphs (i)(9) and (i)(10) of this section.

2. If the alternative disclosure permitted by Note 1 to this paragraph is not applicable because the parent company has independent assets or operations, the condensed consolidating financial information described in paragraph (f)(4) may omit the column for "any other subsidiaries of the parent company on a combined basis" if those other subsidiaries are minor.

3. If any of the subsidiary guarantees is not joint and several with the guarantees of the other subsidiaries, then each subsidiary guarantor whose guarantee is not joint and several need not include separate financial statements, but the condensed consolidating financial information must include a separate column for each subsidiary guarantor whose guarantee is not joint and several.

(g) Recently acquired subsidiary issuers or subsidiary guarantors. (1) The Securities Act registration statement of the parent company must include the financial statements specified in paragraph (g)(2) of this section for any subsidiary that otherwise meets the conditions in paragraph (c), (d), (e) or (f) of this section for omission of separate financial statements if:

(i) The subsidiary has not been included in the audited consolidated results of the parent company for at least nine months of the most recent fiscal year; and

(ii) The net book value or purchase price, whichever is greater, of the subsidiary is 20% or more of the principal amount of the securities being registered.

(2) Financial statements required.

(i) Audited financial statements for a subsidiary described in paragraph (g)(1) of this section must be filed for the subsidiary's most recent fiscal year preceding the acquisition. In addition, unaudited financial statements must be filed for any interim periods specified in §§210.3-01 and 210.3-02.

(ii) The financial statements must conform to the requirements of Regulation S-X (§§210.1-01 through 12-29), except that supporting schedules need not be filed. If the subsidiary is a foreign business, financial statements of the subsidiary meeting the requirements of Item 17 of Form 20-F (§249.220f) will satisfy this item.

(3) Instructions to paragraph (g).

(i) The significance test of paragraph (g)(1)(ii) of this section should be computed using net book value of the subsidiary as of the most recent fiscal year end preceding the acquisition.

(ii) Information required by this paragraph (g) is not required to be included in an annual report or quarterly report.

(iii) Acquisitions of a group of subsidiary issuers or subsidiary guarantors that are related prior to their acquisition shall be aggregated for purposes of applying the 20% test in paragraph (g)(1)(ii) of this section. Subsidiaries shall be deemed to be related prior to their acquisition if:

(A) They are under common control or management;

(B) The acquisition of one subsidiary is conditioned on the acquisition of each subsidiary; or

(C) The acquisition of each subsidiary is conditioned on a single common event.

(h) Definitions. For the purposes of this section:

(1) A subsidiary is "100% owned" if all of its outstanding voting shares are owned, either directly or indirectly, by its parent company. A subsidiary not in corporate form is 100% owned if the sum of all interests are owned, either directly or indirectly, by its parent company other than:

(i) Securities that are guaranteed by its parent and, if applicable, other 100%-owned subsidiaries of its parent; and

(ii) Securities that guarantee securities issued by its parent and, if applicable, other 100%-owned subsidiaries of its parent.

(2) A guarantee is "full and unconditional," if, when an issuer of a guaranteed security has failed to make a scheduled payment, the guarantor is obligated to make the scheduled payment immediately and, if it doesn't, any holder of the guaranteed security may immediately bring suit directly against the guarantor for payment of all amounts due and payable.

(3) Annual report refers to an annual report on Form 10-K or Form 20-F (§249.310 or §249.220f of this chapter).

(4) Quarterly report refers to a quarterly report on Form 10-Q (§249.308a of this chapter).

(5) A parent company has no independent assets or operations if each of its total assets, revenues, income from continuing operations before income taxes, and cash flows from operating activities

(excluding amounts related to its investment in its consolidated subsidiaries) is less than 3% of the corresponding consolidated amount.

(6) A subsidiary is minor if each of its total assets, stockholders' equity, revenues, income from continuing operations before income taxes, and cash flows from operating activities is less than 3% of the parent company's corresponding consolidated amount.

Note to paragraph (h)(6). When considering a group of subsidiaries, the definition applies to each subsidiary in that group individually and to all subsidiaries in that group in the aggregate.

(7) A subsidiary is a finance subsidiary if it has no assets, operations, revenues or cash flows other than those related to the issuance, administration and repayment of the security being registered and any other securities guaranteed by its parent company.

(8) A subsidiary is an operating subsidiary if it is not a finance subsidiary.

(i) Instructions for preparation of condensed consolidating financial information required by paragraphs (c), (d), (e) and (f) of this section.

(1) Follow the general guidance in §210.10-01 for the form and content for condensed financial statements and present the financial information in sufficient detail to allow investors to determine the assets, results of operations and cash flows of each of the consolidating groups;

(2) The financial information should be audited for the same periods that the parent company financial statements are required to be audited;

(3) The parent company column should present investments in all subsidiaries based upon their proportionate share of the subsidiary's net assets;

(4) The parent company's basis shall be "pushed down" to the applicable subsidiary columns to the extent that push down would be required or permitted in separate financial statements of the subsidiary;

(5) All subsidiary issuer or subsidiary guarantor columns should present the following investments in subsidiaries under the equity method:

(i) Non-guarantor subsidiaries;

(ii) Subsidiary issuers or subsidiary guarantors that are not 100% owned or whose guarantee is not full and unconditional;

(iii) Subsidiary guarantors whose guarantee is not joint and several with the guarantees of the other subsidiaries; and

(iv) Subsidiary guarantors with differences in domestic or foreign laws that affect the enforceability of the guarantees;

(6) Provide a separate column for each subsidiary issuer or subsidiary guarantor that is not 100% owned, whose guarantee is not full and unconditional, or whose guarantee is not joint and several with the guarantees of other subsidiaries. Inclusion of a separate column does not relieve that issuer or guarantor from the requirement to file separate financial statements under paragraph (a) of this section. However, paragraphs (b) through (f) of this section will provide this relief if the particular paragraph is satisfied except that the guarantee is not joint and several;

(7) Provide separate columns for each guarantor by legal jurisdiction if differences in domestic or foreign laws affect the enforceability of the guarantees;

(8) Include the following disclosure, if true:

(i) Each subsidiary issuer or subsidiary guarantor is 100% owned by the parent company;

(ii) All guarantees are full and unconditional; and

(iii) Where there is more than one guarantor, all guarantees are joint and several;

(9) Disclose any significant restrictions on the ability of the parent company or any guarantor to obtain funds from its subsidiaries by dividend or loan;

(10) Provide the disclosures prescribed by §210.4-08(e)(3) with respect to the subsidiary issuers and subsidiary guarantors;

(11) The disclosure:

(i) May not omit any financial and narrative information about each guarantor if the information would be material for investors to evaluate the sufficiency of the guarantee;

(ii) Shall include sufficient information so as to make the financial information presented not misleading; and

(iii) Need not repeat information that would substantially duplicate disclosure elsewhere in the parent company's consolidated financial statements; and

(12) Where the parent company's consolidated financial statements are prepared on a comprehensive basis other than U.S. Generally Accepted Accounting Principles or International Financial Reporting Standards as issued by the International Accounting Standards Board, reconcile the information in each column to U.S. Generally Accepted Accounting Principles to the extent necessary to allow investors to evaluate the sufficiency of the guarantees. The reconciliation may be limited to the information specified by Item 17 of Form 20-F (§249.220f of this chapter). The reconciling information need not duplicate information included elsewhere in the reconciliation of the consolidated financial statements.

[65 FR 51707, Aug. 24, 2000, as amended at 73 FR 952, Jan. 4, 2008; 73 FR 1009, Jan. 4, 2008; 74 FR 18615, Apr. 23, 2009]

§210.3-11 Financial statements of an inactive registrant.

If a registrant is an inactive entity as defined below, the financial statements required by this regulation for purposes of reports pursuant to the Securities Exchange Act of 1934 may be unaudited. An inactive entity is one meeting all of the following conditions:

(a) Gross receipts from all sources for the fiscal year are not in excess of $100,000;

(b) The registrant has not purchased or sold any of its own stock, granted options therefor, or levied assessments upon outstanding stock,

(c) Expenditures for all purposes for the fiscal year are not in excess of $100,000;

(d) No material change in the business has occurred during the fiscal year, including any bankruptcy, reorganization, readjustment or succession or any material acquisition or disposition of plants, mines, mining equipment, mine rights or leases; and

(e) No exchange upon which the shares are listed, or governmental authority having jurisdiction, requires the furnishing to it or the publication of audited financial statements.

§210.3-12 Age of financial statements at effective date of registration statement or at mailing date of proxy statement.

(a) If the financial statements in a filing are as of a date the number of days specified in paragraph (g) of this section or more before the date the filing is expected to become effective, or proposed mailing date in the case of a proxy statement, the financial statements shall be updated, except as specified in the following paragraphs, with a balance sheet as of an interim date within the number of days specified in paragraph (g) of this section and with statements of income and cash flows for the interim period between the end of the most recent fiscal year and the date of the interim balance sheet provided and for the corresponding period of the preceding fiscal year. Such interim financial statements may be unaudited and need not be presented in greater detail than is required by §210.10-01. Notwithstanding the above requirements, the most recent interim financial statements shall be at least as current as the most recent financial statements filed with the Commission on Form 10-Q.

(b) Where the anticipated effective date of a filing, or in the case of a proxy statement the proposed mailing date, falls within the number of days subsequent to the end of the fiscal year specified in paragraph (g) of this section, the filing need not include financial statements more current than as of the end of the third fiscal quarter of the most recently completed fiscal year unless the audited financial statements for such fiscal year are available or unless the anticipated effective date or proposed mailing date falls after 45 days subsequent to the end of the fiscal year and the registrant does not meet the conditions prescribed under paragraph (c) of §210.3-01. If the anticipated effective date or proposed mailing date falls after 45 days subsequent to the end of the fiscal year and the registrant does not meet the conditions prescribed under paragraph (c) of §210.3-01, the filing must include audited financial statements for the most recently completed fiscal year.

(c) Where a filing is made near the end of a fiscal year and audited financial statements for that fiscal year are not included in the filing, the filing shall be updated with such audited financial statements if they become available prior to the anticipated effective date, or proposed mailing date in the case of a proxy statement.

(d) The age of the registrant's most recent audited financial statements included in a registration statement filed under the Securities Act of 1933 or filed on Form 10 (17 CFR 249.210) under the Securities Exchange Act of 1934 shall not be more than one year and 45 days old at the date the registration statement becomes effective if the registration statement relates to the security of an issuer that was not subject, immediately before the time of filing the registration statement, to the reporting requirements of section 13 or 15(d) of the Securities Exchange Act of 1934.

(e) For filings by registered management investment companies, the requirements of §210.3-18 shall apply in lieu of the requirements of this section.

(f) Any foreign private issuer may file financial statements whose age is specified in Item 8.A of Form 20-F (§249.220f of this chapter). Financial statements of a foreign business which are furnished pursuant to §210.3-05 or §210.3-09 because it is an acquired business or a 50 percent or less owned person may be of the age specified in Item 8.A of Form 20-F.

(g)(1) For purposes of paragraph (a) of this section, the number of days shall be:

(i) 130 days for large accelerated filers and accelerated filers (as defined in §240.12b-2 of this chapter); and

(ii) 135 days for all other registrants.

(2) For purposes of paragraph (b) of this section, the number of days shall be:

(i) 60 days (75 days for fiscal years ending before December 15, 2006) for large accelerated filers (as defined in §240.12b-2 of this chapter);

(ii) 75 days for accelerated filers (as defined in §240.12b-2 of this chapter); and

(iii) 90 days for all other registrants.

[45 FR 62687, Sept. 25, 1980]

Editorial Note: For Federal Register citations affecting §210.3-12, see the List of CFR Sections Affected, which appears in the Finding Aids section of the printed volume and at www.fdsys.gov.

§210.3-13 Filing of other financial statements in certain cases.

The Commission may, upon the informal written request of the registrant, and where consistent with the protection of investors, permit the omission of one or more of the financial statements herein required or the filing in substitution therefor of appropriate statements of comparable character. The Commission may also by informal written notice require the filing of other financial statements in addition to, or in substitution for, the statements herein required in any case where such statements are necessary or appropriate for an adequate presentation of the financial condition of any person whose financial statements are required, or whose statements are otherwise necessary for the protection of investors.

§210.3-14 Special instructions for real estate operations to be acquired.

(a) If, during the period for which income statements are required, the registrant has acquired one or more properties which in the aggregate are significant, or since the date of the latest balance sheet required has acquired or proposes to acquire one or more properties which in the aggregate are significant, the following shall be furnished with respect to such properties:

(1) Audited income statements (not including earnings per unit) for the three most recent fiscal years, which shall exclude items not comparable to the proposed future operations of the property such as mortgage interest, leasehold rental, depreciation, corporate expenses and Federal and state income taxes: Provided, however, That such audited statements need be presented for only the most recent fiscal year if

(i) The property is not acquired from a related party;

(ii) Material factors considered by the registrant in assessing the property are described with specificity in the filing with regard to the property, including sources of revenue (including, but not limited to, competition in the rental market, comparative rents, occupancy rates) and expense (including, but not limited to, utility rates, ad valorem tax rates, maintenance expenses, capital improvements anticipated); and

(iii) The registrant indicates in the appropriate filing that, after reasonable inquiry, the registrant is not aware of any material factors relating to that specific property other than those discussed in response to paragraph (a)(1)(ii) of this section that would cause the reported financial information not to be necessarily indicative of future operating results.

Note: The discussion of material factors considered should be combined with that required by Item 15 of Form S-11.

(2) If the property is to be operated by the registrant, there shall be furnished a statement showing the estimated taxable operating results of the registrant based on the most recent twelve month period including such adjustments as can be factually supported. If the property is to be acquired subject to a net lease the estimated taxable operating results shall be based on the rent to be paid for the first year of the lease. In either case, the estimated amount of cash to be made available by operations shall be shown. There shall be stated in an introductory paragraph the

principal assumptions which have been made in preparing the statements of estimated taxable operating results and cash to be made available by operations.

(3) If appropriate under the circumstances, there shall be given in tablular form for a limited number of years the estimated cash distribution per unit showing the portion thereof reportable as taxable income and the portion representing a return of capital together with an explanation of annual variations, if any. If taxable net income per unit will become greater than the cash available for distribution per unit, that fact and approximate year of occurrence shall be stated, if significant.

(b) Information required by this section is not required to be included in a filing on Form 10-K.

[45 FR 63687, Sept. 25, 1980, as amended at 47 FR 25122, June 10, 1982; 73 FR 953, Jan. 4, 2008]

§210.3-15   Special provisions as to real estate investment trusts.

(a)(1) The income statement prepared pursuant to §210.5-03 shall include the following additional captions between those required by §210.5-03.15 and 16: (i) Income or loss before gain or loss on sale of properties, extraordinary items and cumulative effects of accounting changes, and (ii) gain or loss on sale of properties, less applicable income tax.

(2) The balance sheet required by §210.5-02 shall set forth in lieu of the captions required by §210.5-02.31(a)(3): (i) The balance of undistributed income from other than gain or loss on sale of properties and (ii) accumulated undistributed net realized gain or loss on sale of properties. The information specified in §210.3-04 shall be modified similarly.

(b) The trust's status as a real estate investment trust under applicable provisions of the Internal Revenue Code as amended shall be stated in a note referred to in the appropriate statements. Such note shall also indicate briefly the principal present assumptions on which the trust has relied in making or not making provisons for Federal income taxes.

(c) The tax status of distributions per unit shall be stated (e.g., ordinary income, capital gain, return of capital).

[45 FR 63687, Sept. 25, 1980, as amended at 50 FR 49532, Dec. 3, 1985]

§210.3-16   Financial statements of affiliates whose securities collateralize an issue registered or being registered.

(a) For each of the registrant's affiliates whose securities constitute a substantial portion of the collateral for any class of securities registered or being registered, there shall be filed the financial statements that would be required if the affiliate were a registrant and required to file financial statements. However, financial statements need not be filed pursuant to this section for any person whose statements are otherwise separately included in the filing on an individual basis or on a basis consolidated with its subsidiaries.

(b) For the purposes of this section, securities of a person shall be deemed to constitute a substantial portion of collateral if the aggregate principal amount, par value, or book value of the securities as carried by the registrant, or the market value of such securities, whichever is the greatest, equals 20 percent or more of the principal amount of the secured class of securities.

[65 FR 51710, Aug. 24, 2000]

§210.3-17 Financial statements of natural persons.

(a) In lieu of the financial statements otherwise required, a natural person may file an unaudited balance sheet as of a date within 90 days of date of filing and unaudited statements of income for each of the three most recent fiscal years.

(b) Financial statements conforming with the instructions as to financial statements of subsidiaries not consolidated and 50 percent or less owned persons under §210.3-09(a) shall be separately presented for: (1) Each business owned as a sole proprietor, (2) each partnership, business trust, unincorporated association, or similar business organization of which the person holds a controlling interest and (3) each corporation of which the person, directly or indirectly, owns securities representing more than 50 percent of the voting power.

(c) Separate financial statements may be omitted, however, for each corporation, business trust, unincorporated association, or similar business organization if the person's total investment in such entity does not exceed 5 percent of his total assets and the person's total income from such entity does not exceed 5 percent of his gross income; Provided, that the person's aggregate investment in and income from all such omitted entities shall not exceed 15 percent of his total assets and gross income, respectively.

[46 FR 12491, Feb. 17, 1981, as amended at 50 FR 25215, June 18, 1985]

§210.3-18 Special provisions as to registered management investment companies and companies required to be registered as management investment companies.

(a) For filings by registered management investment companies, the following financial statements shall be filed:

(1) An audited balance sheet or statement of assets and liabilities as of the end of the most recent fiscal year;

(2) An audited statement of operations for the most recent fiscal year conforming to the requirements of §210.6-07.

(3) An audited statement of cash flows for the most recent fiscal year if necessary to comply with generally accepted accounting principles. (Further references in this rule to the requirement for such statement are likewise applicable only to the extent that they are consistent with the requirements of generally accepted accounting principles.)

(4) Audited statements of changes in net assets conforming to the requirements of §210.6-09 for the two most recent fiscal years.

(b) If the filing is made within 60 days after the end of the registrant's fiscal year and audited financial statements for the most recent fiscal year are not available, the balance sheet or statement of assets and liabilities may be as of the end of the preceding fiscal year and the filing shall include an additional balance sheet or statement of assets and liabilities as of an interim date within 245 days of the date of filing. In addition, the statements of operations and cash flows (if required by generally accepted accounting principles) shall be provided for the preceding fiscal year and the statement of changes in net assets shall be provided for the two preceding fiscal years and each of the statements shall be provided for the interim period between the end of the preceding fiscal year and the date of the most recent balance sheet or statement of assets and liabilities being filed. Financial statements for the corresponding period of the preceding fiscal year need not be provided.

(c) If the most current balance sheet or statement of assets and liabilities in a filing is as of a date 245 days or more prior to the date the filing is expected to become effective, the financial statements shall be updated with a balance sheet or statement of assets and liabilities as of an interim date within 245 days. In addition, the statements of operations, cash flows, and changes in net assets shall be provided for the interim period between the end of the most recent fiscal year for which a balance sheet or statement of assets and liabilities is presented and the date of the most recent interim balance sheet or statement of assets and liabilities filed.

(d) Interim financial statements provided in accordance with these requirements may be unaudited but shall be presented in the same detail as required by §§210.6-01 to 210.6-10. When unaudited financial statements are presented in a registration statement, they shall include the statement required by §210.3-03(d).

[46 FR 36125, July 14, 1981; 46 FR 46795, Sept. 22, 1981, as amended at 47 FR 29837, July 9, 1982; 47 FR 56838, Dec. 21, 1982; 57 FR 45292, Oct. 1, 1992; 76 FR 71875, Nov. 21, 2011]

§210.3-19   [Reserved]

§210.3-20   Currency for financial statements of foreign private issuers.
(a) A foreign private issuer, as defined in §230.405 of this chapter, shall state amounts in its primary financial statements in the currency which it deems appropriate.

(b) The currency in which amounts in the financial statements are stated shall be disclosed prominently on the face of the financial statements. If dividends on publicly-held equity securities will be declared in a currency other than the reporting currency, a note to the financial statements shall identify that currency. If there are material exchange restrictions or controls relating to the issuer's reporting currency, the currency of the issuer's domicile, or the currency in which the issuer will pay dividends, prominent disclosure of this fact shall be made in the financial statements. If the reporting currency is not the U.S. dollar, dollar-equivalent financial statements or convenience translations shall not be presented, except a translation may be presented of the most recent fiscal year and any subsequent interim period presented using the exchange rate as of the most recent balance sheet included in the filing, except that a rate as of the most recent practicable date shall be used if materially different.

(c) If the financial statements of a foreign private issuer are stated in a currency of a country that has experienced cumulative inflationary effects exceeding a total of 100 percent over the most recent three year period, and have not been recast or otherwise supplemented to include information on a historical cost/constant currency or current cost basis prescribed or permitted by appropriate authoritative standards, the issuer shall present supplementary information to quantify the effects of changing prices upon its financial position and results of operations.

(d) Notwithstanding the currency selected for reporting purposes, the issuer shall measure separately its own transactions, and those of each of its material operations (e.g., branches, divisions, subsidiaries, joint ventures, and similar entities) that is included in the issuer's consolidated financial statements and not located in a hyperinflationary environment, using the particular currency of the primary economic environment in which the issuer or the operation conducts its business. Assets and liabilities so determined shall be translated into the reporting currency at the exchange rate at the balance sheet date; all revenues, expenses, gains, and losses shall be translated at the exchange rate existing at the time of the transaction or, if appropriate, a weighted average of the exchange rates during the period; and all translation effects of exchange rate changes shall be included as a separate component ("cumulative translation adjustment") of shareholder's equity. For purposes of this paragraph, the currency of an operation's primary economic environment is normally the currency in which cash is primarily generated and expended; a hyperinflationary environment is one that has cumulative inflation of approximately 100% or more over the most recent three year period. Departures from the methodology presented in this paragraph shall be quantified pursuant to Item 17(c)(2) of Form 20-F (§249.220f of this chapter).

(e) The issuer shall state its primary financial statements in the same currency for all periods for which financial information is presented. If the financial statements are stated in a currency that is different from that used in financial statements previously filed with the Commission, the issuer shall recast its financial statements as if the newly adopted currency had been used since at least the earliest period presented in the filing. The decision to change and the reason for the change in the reporting currency shall be disclosed in a note to the financial statements in the period in which the change occurs.

[59 FR 65631, Dec. 20, 1994, as amended at 64 FR 53908, Oct. 5, 1999]

Consolidated and Combined Financial Statements

§210.3A-01   Application of §210.3A-01 to §210.3A-05.
Sections 210.3A-01 to 210.3A-05 shall govern the presentation of consolidated and combined financial statements.

[44 FR 19386, Apr. 3, 1979. Redesignated at 45 FR 63687, Sept. 25, 1980, and amended at 50 FR 25215, June 18, 1985]

§210.3A-02 Consolidated financial statements of the registrant and its subsidiaries.

In deciding upon consolidation policy, the registrant must consider what financial presentation is most meaningful in the circumstances and should follow in the consolidated financial statements principles of inclusion or exclusion which will clearly exhibit the financial position and results of operations of the registrant. There is a presumption that consolidated statements are more meaningful than separate statements and that they are usually necessary for a fair presentation when one entity directly or indirectly has a controlling financial interest in another entity. Other particular facts and circumstances may require combined financial statements, an equity method of accounting, or valuation allowances in order to achieve a fair presentation. In any case, the disclosures required by §210.3A-03 should clearly explain the accounting policies followed by the registrant in this area, including the circumstances involved in any departure from the normal practice of consolidating majority owned subsidiaries and not consolidating entities that are less than majority owned. Among the factors that the registrant should consider in determining the most meaningful presentation are the following:

(a) Majority ownership: Generally, registrants shall consolidate entities that are majority owned and shall not consolidate entities that are not majority owned. The determination of majority ownership requires a careful analysis of the facts and circumstances of a particular relationship among entities. In rare situations, consolidation of a majority owned subsidiary may not result in a fair presentation, because the registrant, in substance, does not have a controlling financial interest (for example, when the subsidiary is in legal reorganization or in bankruptcy). In other situations, consolidation of an entity, notwithstanding the lack of technical majority ownership, is necessary to present fairly the financial position and results of operations of the registrant, because of the existence of a parent-subsidiary relationship by means other than record ownership of voting stock.

(b) Different fiscal periods: Generally, registrants shall not consolidate any entity whose financial statements are as of a date or for periods substantially different from those of the registrant. Rather, the earnings or losses of such entities should be reflected in the registrant's financial statements on the equity method of accounting. However:

(1) A difference in fiscal periods does not of itself justify the exclusion of an entity from consolidation. It ordinarily is feasible for such entity to prepare, for consolidation purposes, statements for a period which corresponds with or closely approaches the fiscal year of the registrant. Where the difference is not more than 93 days, it is usually acceptable to use, for consolidation purposes, such entity's statements for its fiscal period. Such difference, when it exists, should be disclosed as follows: the closing date of the entity should be expressly indicated, and the necessity for the use of different closing dates should be briefly explained. Furthermore, recognition should be given by disclosure or otherwise to the effect of intervening events which materially affect the financial position or results of operations.

(2) Notwithstanding the 93-day provision specified in paragraph (b)(1) of this section, in connection with the retroactive combination of financial statements of entities following a combination between entities under common control, the financial statements of the constituents may be combined even if their respective fiscal periods do not end within 93 days, except that the financial statements for the latest fiscal year shall be recast to dates which do not differ by more than 93 days, if practicable. Disclosure shall be made of the periods combined and of the sales or revenues, net income before extraordinary items and net income of any interim periods excluded from or included more than once in results of operations as a result of such recasting.

(c) Bank Holding Company Act: Registrants shall not consolidate any subsidiary or group of subsidiaries of a registrant subject to the Bank Holding Company Act of 1956 as amended as to which (1) a decision requiring divestiture has been made, or (2) there is substantial likelihood that divestiture will be necessary in order to comply with provisions of the Bank Holding Company Act.

(d) Foreign subsidiaries: Due consideration shall be given to the propriety of consolidating with domestic corporations foreign subsidiaries which are operated under political, economic or currency restrictions. If consolidated, disclosure should be made as to the effect, insofar as this can reasonably be determined, of foreign exchange restrictions upon the consolidated financial position and operating results of the registrant and its subsidiaries.

[51 FR 17330, May 12, 1986, as amended at 74 FR 18615, Apr. 23, 2009]

§210.3A-03 Statement as to principles of consolidation or combination followed.

(a) A brief description of the principles followed in consolidating or combining the separate financial statements, including the principles followed in determining the inclusion or exclusion of (1) subsidiaries in consolidated or combined financial statements and (2) companies in consolidated or combined financial statements, shall be stated in the notes to the respective financial statements.

(b) As to each consolidated financial statement and as to each combined financial statement, if there has been a change in the persons included or excluded in the corresponding statement for the preceding fiscal period filed with the Commission which has a material effect on the financial statements, the persons included and the persons excluded shall be disclosed. If there have been any changes in the respective fiscal periods of the persons included made during the periods of the report which have a material effect on the financial statements, indicate clearly such changes and the manner of treatment.

[37 FR 14597, July 21, 1972. Redesignated at 45 FR 63687, Sept. 25, 1980, and 46 FR 56179, Nov. 16, 1981]

§210.3A-04 Intercompany items and transactions.

In general, there shall be eliminated intercompany items and transactions between persons included in the (a) consolidated financial statements being filed and, as appropriate, (b) unrealized intercompany profits and losses on transactions between persons for which financial statements are being filed and persons the investment in which is presented in such statements by the equity method. If such eliminations are not made, a statement of the reasons and the methods of treatment shall be made.

[37 FR 14597, July 21, 1972. Redesignated at 46 FR 56179, Nov. 16, 1981]

Rules of General Application
Source: Sections 210.4-01 through 210.4-10 appear at 45 FR 63669, Sept. 25, 1980, unless otherwise noted.

§210.4-01   Form, order, and terminology.
(a) Financial statements should be filed in such form and order, and should use such generally accepted terminology, as will best indicate their significance and character in the light of the provisions applicable thereto. The information required with respect to any statement shall be furnished as a minimum requirement to which shall be added such further material information as is necessary to make the required statements, in the light of the circumstances under which they are made, not misleading.

(1) Financial statements filed with the Commission which are not prepared in accordance with generally accepted accounting principles will be presumed to be misleading or inaccurate, despite footnote or other disclosures, unless the Commission has otherwise provided. This article and other articles of Regulation S-X provide clarification of certain disclosures which must be included in any event, in financial statements filed with the Commission.

(2) In all filings of foreign private issuers (see §230.405 of this chapter), except as stated otherwise in the applicable form, the financial statements may be prepared according to a comprehensive set of accounting principles, other than those generally accepted in the United States or International Financial Reporting Standards as issued by the International Accounting Standards Board, if a reconciliation to U.S. Generally Accepted Accounting Principles and the provisions of Regulation S-X of the type specified in Item 18 of Form 20-F (§249.220f of this chapter) is also filed as part of the financial statements. Alternatively, the financial statements may be prepared according to U.S. Generally Accepted Accounting Principles or International Financial Reporting Standards as issued by the International Accounting Standards Board.

(3)(i) Notwithstanding the effective dates set forth in FASB ASC Topic 718, Compensation—Stock Compensation", financial statements shall be prepared in accordance with FASB ASC Topic 718 beginning with:

(A) The first interim or annual reporting period of the registrant's first fiscal year beginning on or after June 15, 2005, provided the registrant does not file as a smaller reporting company; and

(B) The first interim or annual reporting period of the registrant's first fiscal year beginning on or after December 15, 2005, provided the registrant files as a smaller reporting company.

(ii) For periods prior to the effective dates set forth in this paragraph, FASB ASC Topic 718 and prior authoritative guidance, shall be considered to be generally accepted accounting principles.

(b) All money amounts required to be shown in financial statements may be expressed in whole dollars or multiples thereof, as appropriate: Provided, That, when stated in other than whole dollars, an indication to that effect is inserted immediately beneath the caption of the statement or schedule, at the top of the money columns, or at an appropriate point in narrative material.

(c) Negative amounts (red figures) shall be shown in a manner which clearly distinguishes the negative attribute. When determining methods of display, consideration should be given to the limitations of reproduction and microfilming processes.

[45 FR 63669, Sept. 25, 1980, as amended at 47 FR 54767, Dec. 6, 1982; 70 FR 20719, Apr. 21, 2005; 73 FR 953, Jan. 4, 2008; 73 FR 1009, Jan. 4, 2008; 76 FR 50119, Aug. 12, 2011]

§210.4-02 Items not material.

If the amount which would otherwise be required to be shown with respect to any item is not material, it need not be separately set forth. The combination of insignificant amounts is permitted.

§210.4-03 Inapplicable captions and omission of unrequired or inapplicable financial statements.

(a) No caption should be shown in any financial statement as to which the items and conditions are not present.

(b) Financial statements not required or inapplicable because the required matter is not present need not be filed.

(c) The reasons for the omission of any required financial statements shall be indicated.

§210.4-04 Omission of substantially identical notes.

If a note covering substantially the same subject matter is required with respect to two or more financial statements relating to the same or affiliated persons, for which separate sets of notes are presented, the required information may be shown in a note to only one of such statements: Provided, that a clear and specific reference thereto is made in each of the other statements with respect to which the note is required.

§§210.4-05--210.4-06 [Reserved]

§210.4-07 Discount on shares.

Discount on shares, or any unamortized balance thereof, shall be shown separately as a deduction from the applicable account(s) as circumstances require.

§210.4-08 General notes to financial statements.

If applicable to the person for which the financial statements are filed, the following shall be set forth on the face of the appropriate statement or in appropriately captioned notes. The information shall be provided for each statement required to be filed, except that the information required by paragraphs (b), (c), (d), (e) and (f) shall be provided as of the most recent audited balance sheet being filed and for paragraph (j) as specified therein. When specific statements are presented separately, the pertinent notes shall accompany such statements unless cross-referencing is appropriate.

(a) Principles of consolidation or combination. With regard to consolidated or combined financial statements, refer to §§210.3A-01 to 3A-08 for requirements for supplemental information in notes to the financial statements.

(b) Assets subject to lien. Assets mortgaged, pledged, or otherwise subject to lien, and the approximate amounts thereof, shall be designated and the obligations collateralized briefly identified.

(c) Defaults. The facts and amounts concerning any default in principal, interest, sinking fund, or redemption provisions with respect to any issue of securities or credit agreements, or any breach of covenant of a related indenture or agreement, which default or breach existed at the date of the most recent balance sheet being filed and which has not been subsequently cured, shall be stated in the notes to the financial statements. If a default or breach exists but acceleration of the obligation has been waived for a stated period of time beyond the date of the most recent balance sheet being filed, state the amount of the obligation and the period of the waiver.

(d) Preferred shares. (1) Aggregate preferences on involuntary liquidation, if other than par or stated value, shall be shown parenthetically in the equity section of the balance sheet.

(2) Disclosure shall be made of any restriction upon retained earnings that arises from the fact that upon involuntary liquidation the aggregate preferences of the preferred shares exceeds the par or stated value of such shares.

(e) Restrictions which limit the payment of dividends by the registrant. (1) Describe the most significant restrictions, other than as reported under paragraph (d) of this section, on the payment of dividends by the registrant, indicating their sources, their pertinent provisions, and the amount of retained earnings or net income restricted or free of restrictions.

(2) Disclose the amount of consolidated retained earnings which represents undistributed earnings of 50 percent or less owned persons accounted for by the equity method.

(3) The disclosures in paragraphs (e)(3) (i) and (ii) in this section shall be provided when the restricted net assets of consolidated and unconsolidated subsidiaries and the parent's equity in the

56

undistributed earnings of 50 percent or less owned persons accounted for by the equity method together exceed 25 percent of consolidated net assets as of the end of the most recently completed fiscal year. For purposes of this test, restricted net assets of subsidiaries shall mean that amount of the registrant's proportionate share of net assets (after intercompany eliminations) reflected in the balance sheets of its consolidated and unconsolidated subsidiaries as of the end of the most recent fiscal year which may not be transferred to the parent company in the form of loans, advances or cash dividends by the subsidiaries without the consent of a third party (i.e., lender, regulatory agency, foreign government, etc.). Not all limitations on transferability of assets are considered to be restrictions for purposes of this test, which considers only specific third party restrictions on the ability of subsidiaries to transfer funds outside of the entity. For example, the presence of subsidiary debt which is secured by certain of the subsidiary's assets does not constitute a restriction under this rule. However, if there are any loan provisions prohibiting dividend payments, loans or advances to the parent by a subsidiary, these are considered restrictions for purposes of computing restricted net assets. When a loan agreement requires that a subsidiary maintain certain working capital, net tangible asset, or net asset levels, or where formal compensating arrangements exist, there is considered to be a restriction under the rule because the lender's intent is normally to preclude the transfer by dividend or otherwise of funds to the parent company. Similarly, a provision which requires that a subsidiary reinvest all of its earnings is a restriction, since this precludes loans, advances or dividends in the amount of such undistributed earnings by the entity. Where restrictions on the amount of funds which may be loaned or advanced differ from the amount restricted as to transfer in the form of cash dividends, the amount least restrictive to the subsidiary shall be used. Redeemable preferred stocks (§210.5-02.27) and noncontrolling interests shall be deducted in computing net assets for purposes of this test.

(i) Describe the nature of any restrictions on the ability of consolidated subsidiaries and unconsolidated subsidiaries to transfer funds to the registrant in the form of cash dividends, loans or advances (i.e., borrowing arrangements, regulatory restraints, foreign government, etc.).

(ii) Disclose separately the amounts of such restricted net assets for unconsolidated subsidiaries and consolidated subsidiaries as of the end of the most recently completed fiscal year.

(f) Significant changes in bonds, mortgages and similar debt. Any significant changes in the authorized or issued amounts of bonds, mortgages and similar debt since the date of the latest balance sheet being filed for a particular person or group shall be stated.

(g) Summarized financial information of subsidiaries not consolidated and 50 percent or less owned persons. (1) The summarized information as to assets, liabilities and results of operations as detailed in §210.1-02(bb) shall be presented in notes to the financial statements on an individual or group basis for:

(i) Subsidiaries not consolidated; or

(ii) For 50 percent or less owned persons accounted for by the equity method by the registrant or by a subsidiary of the registrant, if the criteria in §210.1-02(w) for a significant subsidiary are met:

(A) Individually by any subsidiary not consolidated or any 50% or less owned person; or

(B) On an aggregated basis by any combination of such subsidiaries and persons.

(2) Summarized financial information shall be presented insofar as is practicable as of the same dates and for the same periods as the audited consolidated financial statements provided and shall include the disclosures prescribed by §210.1-02(bb). Summarized information of subsidiaries not consolidated shall not be combined for disclosure purposes with the summarized information of 50 percent or less owned persons.

(h) Income tax expense. (1) Disclosure shall be made in the income statement or a note thereto, of (i) the components of income (loss) before income tax expense (benefit) as either domestic or foreign; (ii) the components of income tax expense, including (A) taxes currently payable and (B) the net tax effects, as applicable, of timing differences (indicate separately the amount of the estimated tax effect of each of the various types of timing differences, such as depreciation, warranty costs, etc., where the amount of each such tax effect exceeds five percent of the amount computed by multiplying the income before tax by the applicable statutory Federal income tax rate; other differences may be combined.)

Note: Amounts applicable to United States Federal income taxes, to foreign income taxes and the other income taxes shall be stated separately for each major component. Amounts applicable to foreign income (loss) and amounts applicable to foreign or other income taxes which are less than five percent of the total of income before taxes or the component of tax expense, respectively, need not be separately disclosed. For purposes of this rule, foreign income (loss) is defined as income (loss) generated from a registrant's foreign operations, i.e., operations that are located outside of the registrant's home country.

(2) Provide a reconciliation between the amount of reported total income tax expense (benefit) and the amount computed by multiplying the income (loss) before tax by the applicable statutory Federal income tax rate, showing the estimated dollar amount of each of the underlying causes for the difference. If no individual reconciling item amounts to more than five percent of the amount computed by multiplying the income before tax by the applicable statutory Federal income tax rate, and the total difference to be reconciled is less than five percent of such computed amount, no reconciliation need be provided unless it would be significant in appraising the trend of earnings. Reconciling items that are individually less than five percent of the computed amount may be aggregated in the reconciliation. The reconciliation may be presented in percentages rather than in dollar amounts. Where the reporting person is a foreign entity, the income tax rate in that person's country of domicile should normally be used in making the above computation, but different rates should not be used for subsidiaries or other segments of a reporting entity. When the rate used by a reporting person is other than the United States Federal corporate income tax rate, the rate used and the basis for using such rate shall be disclosed.

(3) Paragraphs (h) (1) and (2) of this section shall be applied in the following manner to financial statements which reflect the adoption of FASB ASC Topic 740, Income Taxes.

(i) The disclosures required by paragraph (h)(1)(ii) of this section and by the parenthetical instruction at the end of paragraph (h)(1) of this section and by the introductory sentence of paragraph (h)(2) of this section shall not apply.

(ii) The instructional note between paragraphs (h) (1) and (2) of this section and the balance of the requirements of paragraphs (h) (1) and (2) of this section shall continue to apply.

(i) Warrants or rights outstanding. Information with respect to warrants or rights outstanding at the date of the related balance sheet shall be set forth as follows:

(1) Title of issue of securities called for by warrants or rights.

(2) Aggregate amount of securities called for by warrants or rights outstanding.

(3) Date from which warrants or rights are exercisable.

(4) Price at which warrant or right is exercisable.

(j) [Reserved]

(k) Related party transactions which affect the financial statements. (1) Related party transactions should be identified and the amounts stated on the face of the balance sheet, income statement, or statement of cash flows.

(2) In cases where separate financial statements are presented for the registrant, certain investees, or subsidiaries, separate disclosure shall be made in such statements of the amounts in the related consolidated financial statements which are (i) eliminated and (ii) not eliminated. Also, any intercompany profits or losses resulting from transactions with related parties and not eliminated and the effects thereof shall be disclosed.

(l) [Reserved]

(m) Repurchase and reverse repurchase agreements—(1) Repurchase agreements (assets sold under agreements to repurchase). (i) If, as of the most recent balance sheet date, the carrying amount (or market value, if higher than the carrying amount or if there is no carrying amount) of the securities or other assets sold under agreements to repurchase (repurchase agreements) exceeds 10% of total assets, disclose separately in the balance sheet the aggregate amount of liabilities incurred pursuant to repurchase agreements including accrued interest payable thereon.

(ii)(A) If, as of the most recent balance sheet date, the carrying amount (or market value, if higher than the carrying amount) of securities or other assets sold under repurchase agreements, other than securities or assets specified in paragraph (m)(1)(ii)(B) of this section, exceeds 10% of total assets, disclose in an appropriately captioned footnote containing a tabular presentation, segregated as to type of such securities or assets sold under agreements to repurchase (e.g., U.S. Treasury obligations, U.S. Government agency obligations and loans), the following information as of the balance sheet date for each such agreement or group of agreements (other than agreements involving securities or assets specified in paragraph (m)(1)(ii)(B) of this section) maturing (1) overnight; (2) term up to 30 days; (3) term of 30 to 90 days; (4) term over 90 days and (5) demand:

(i) The carrying amount and market value of the assets sold under agreement to repurchase, including accrued interest plus any cash or other assets on deposit under the repurchase agreements; and

(ii) The repurchase liability associated with such transaction or group of transactions and the interest rate(s) thereon.

(B) For purposes of paragraph (m)(1)(ii)(A) of this section only, do not include securities or other assets for which unrealized changes in market value are reported in current income or which have been obtained under reverse repurchase agreements.

(iii) If, as of the most recent balance sheet date, the amount at risk under repurchase agreements with any individual counterparty or group of related counterparties exceeds 10% of stockholders' equity (or in the case of investment companies, net asset value), disclose the name of each such counterparty or group of related counterparties, the amount at risk with each, and the weighted average maturity of the repurchase agreements with each. The amount at risk under repurchase agreements is defined as the excess of carrying amount (or market value, if higher than the carrying amount or if there is no carrying amount) of the securities or other assets sold under agreement to repurchase, including accrued interest plus any cash or other assets on deposit to secure the repurchase obligation, over the amount of the repurchase liability (adjusted for accrued interest). (Cash deposits in connection with repurchase agreements shall not be reported as unrestricted cash pursuant to rule 5-02.1.)

(2) Reverse repurchase agreements (assets purchased under agreements to resell). (i) If, as of the most recent balance sheet date, the aggregate carrying amount of reverse repurchase agreements (securities or other assets purchased under agreements to resell) exceeds 10% of total assets: (A) Disclose separately such amount in the balance sheet; and (B) disclose in an appropriately captioned footnote: (1) The registrant's policy with regard to taking possession of securities or other assets purchased under agreements to resell; and (2) whether or not there are any provisions to ensure that the market value of the underlying assets remains sufficient to protect the registrant in the event of default by the counterparty and if so, the nature of those provisions.

(ii) If, as of the most recent balance sheet date, the amount at risk under reverse repurchase agreements with any individual counterparty or group of related counterparties exceeds 10% of stockholders' equity (or in the case of investment companies, net asset value), disclose the name of each such counterparty or group of related counterparties, the amount at risk with each, and the weighted average maturity of the reverse repurchase agreements with each. The amount at risk under reverse repurchase agreements is defined as the excess of the carrying amount of the reverse repurchase agreements over the market value of assets delivered pursuant to the agreements by the counterparty to the registrant (or to a third party agent that has affirmatively agreed to act on behalf of the registrant) and not returned to the counterparty, exept in exchange for their approximate market value in a separate transaction.

(n) Accounting policies for certain derivative instruments. Disclosures regarding accounting policies shall include descriptions of the accounting policies used for derivative financial instruments and derivative commodity instruments and the methods of applying those policies that materially affect the determination of financial position, cash flows, or results of operation. This description shall include, to the extent material, each of the following items:

(1) A discussion of each method used to account for derivative financial instruments and derivative commodity instruments;

(2) The types of derivative financial instruments and derivative commodity instruments accounted for under each method; (3) The criteria required to be met for each accounting method used, including a discussion of the criteria required to be met for hedge or deferral accounting and accrual or settlement accounting (e.g., whether and how risk reduction, correlation, designation, and effectiveness tests are applied);

(4) The accounting method used if the criteria specified in paragraph (n)(3) of this section are not met;

(5) The method used to account for terminations of derivatives designated as hedges or derivatives used to affect directly or indirectly the terms, fair values, or cash flows of a designated item;

(6) The method used to account for derivatives when the designated item matures, is sold, is extinguished, or is terminated. In addition, the method used to account for derivatives designated to an anticipated transaction, when the anticipated transaction is no longer likely to occur; and

(7) Where and when derivative financial instruments and derivative commodity instruments, and their related gains and losses, are reported in the statements of financial position, cash flows, and results of operations.

Instructions to paragraph (n): 1. For purposes of this paragraph (n), derivative financial instruments and derivative commodity instruments (collectively referred to as "derivatives") are defined as follows:

(i) Derivative financial instruments have the same meaning as defined by generally accepted accounting principles (see, e.g., FASB ASC Master Glossary, and include futures, forwards, swaps, options, and other financial instruments with similar characteristics.

(ii) Derivative commodity instruments include, to the extent such instruments are not derivative financial instruments, commodity futures, commodity forwards, commodity swaps, commodity options, and other commodity instruments with similar characteristics that are permitted by contract or business custom to be settled in cash or with another financial instrument. For purposes of this paragraph, settlement in cash includes settlement in cash of the net change in value of the derivative commodity instrument (e.g., net cash settlement based on changes in the price of the underlying commodity).

61

2. For purposes of paragraphs (n)(2), (n)(3), (n)(4), and (n)(7), the required disclosures should address separately derivatives entered into for trading purposes and derivatives entered into for purposes other than trading. For purposes of this paragraph, trading purposes means dealing and other trading activities measured at fair value with gains and losses recognized in earnings.

3. For purposes of paragraph (n)(6), anticipated transactions means transactions (other than transactions involving existing assets or liabilities or transactions necessitated by existing firm commitments) an enterprise expects, but is not obligated, to carry out in the normal course of business.

4. Registrants should provide disclosures required under paragraph (n) in filings with the Commission that include financial statements of fiscal periods ending after June 15, 1997.

[45 FR 63669, Sept. 25, 1980, as amended at 46 FR 56179, Nov. 16, 1981; 50 FR 25215, June 18, 1985; 50 FR 49532, Dec. 3, 1985; 51 FR 3770, Jan. 30, 1986; 57 FR 45293, Oct. 1, 1992; 59 FR 65636, Dec. 20, 1994; 62 FR 6063, Feb. 10, 1997; 74 FR 18615, Apr. 23, 2009; 76 FR 50119, Aug. 12, 2011]

§210.4-9 [Reserved]

§210.4-10 Financial accounting and reporting for oil and gas producing activities pursuant to the Federal securities laws and the Energy Policy and Conservation Act of 1975.

This section prescribes financial accounting and reporting standards for registrants with the Commission engaged in oil and gas producing activities in filings under the Federal securities laws and for the preparation of accounts by persons engaged, in whole or in part, in the production of crude oil or natural gas in the United States, pursuant to section 503 of the Energy Policy and Conservation Act of 1975 (42 U.S.C. 6383) (EPCA) and section 11(c) of the Energy Supply and Environmental Coordination Act of 1974 (15 U.S.C. 796) (ESECA), as amended by section 505 of EPCA. The application of this section to those oil and gas producing operations of companies regulated for ratemaking purposes on an individual-company-cost-of-service basis may, however, give appropriate recognition to differences arising because of the effect of the ratemaking process.

Exemption. Any person exempted by the Department of Energy from any record-keeping or reporting requirements pursuant to section 11(c) of ESECA, as amended, is similarly exempted from the related provisions of this section in the preparation of accounts pursuant to EPCA. This exemption does not affect the applicability of this section to filings pursuant to the Federal securities laws.

Definitions
(a) Definitions. The following definitions apply to the terms listed below as they are used in this section:

(1) Acquisition of properties. Costs incurred to purchase, lease or otherwise acquire a property, including costs of lease bonuses and options to purchase or lease properties, the portion of costs applicable to minerals when land including mineral rights is purchased in fee, brokers' fees, recording fees, legal costs, and other costs incurred in acquiring properties.

(2) Analogous reservoir. Analogous reservoirs, as used in resources assessments, have similar rock and fluid properties, reservoir conditions (depth, temperature, and pressure) and drive mechanisms, but are typically at a more advanced stage of development than the reservoir of interest and thus may provide concepts to assist in the interpretation of more limited data and estimation of recovery. When used to support proved reserves, an "analogous reservoir" refers to a reservoir that shares the following characteristics with the reservoir of interest:

(i) Same geological formation (but not necessarily in pressure communication with the reservoir of interest);

(ii) Same environment of deposition;

(iii) Similar geological structure; and

(iv) Same drive mechanism.

Instruction to paragraph (a)(2): Reservoir properties must, in the aggregate, be no more favorable in the analog than in the reservoir of interest.

(3) Bitumen. Bitumen, sometimes referred to as natural bitumen, is petroleum in a solid or semi-solid state in natural deposits with a viscosity greater than 10,000 centipoise measured at original temperature in the deposit and atmospheric pressure, on a gas free basis. In its natural state it usually contains sulfur, metals, and other non-hydrocarbons.

(4) Condensate. Condensate is a mixture of hydrocarbons that exists in the gaseous phase at original reservoir temperature and pressure, but that, when produced, is in the liquid phase at surface pressure and temperature.

(5) Deterministic estimate. The method of estimating reserves or resources is called deterministic when a single value for each parameter (from the geoscience, engineering, or economic data) in the reserves calculation is used in the reserves estimation procedure.

(6) Developed oil and gas reserves. Developed oil and gas reserves are reserves of any category that can be expected to be recovered:

(i) Through existing wells with existing equipment and operating methods or in which the cost of the required equipment is relatively minor compared to the cost of a new well; and

(ii) Through installed extraction equipment and infrastructure operational at the time of the reserves estimate if the extraction is by means not involving a well.

(7) Development costs. Costs incurred to obtain access to proved reserves and to provide facilities for extracting, treating, gathering and storing the oil and gas. More specifically, development costs, including depreciation and applicable operating costs of support equipment and facilities and other costs of development activities, are costs incurred to:

(i) Gain access to and prepare well locations for drilling, including surveying well locations for the purpose of determining specific development drilling sites, clearing ground, draining, road building, and relocating public roads, gas lines, and power lines, to the extent necessary in developing the proved reserves.

(ii) Drill and equip development wells, development-type stratigraphic test wells, and service wells, including the costs of platforms and of well equipment such as casing, tubing, pumping equipment, and the wellhead assembly.

(iii) Acquire, construct, and install production facilities such as lease flow lines, separators, treaters, heaters, manifolds, measuring devices, and production storage tanks, natural gas cycling and processing plants, and central utility and waste disposal systems.

(iv) Provide improved recovery systems.

(8) Development project. A development project is the means by which petroleum resources are brought to the status of economically producible. As examples, the development of a single reservoir or field, an incremental development in a producing field, or the integrated development of a group of several fields and associated facilities with a common ownership may constitute a development project.

(9) Development well. A well drilled within the proved area of an oil or gas reservoir to the depth of a stratigraphic horizon known to be productive.

(10) Economically producible. The term economically producible, as it relates to a resource, means a resource which generates revenue that exceeds, or is reasonably expected to exceed, the costs of the operation. The value of the products that generate revenue shall be determined at the terminal point of oil and gas producing activities as defined in paragraph (a)(16) of this section.

(11) Estimated ultimate recovery (EUR). Estimated ultimate recovery is the sum of reserves remaining as of a given date and cumulative production as of that date.

(12) Exploration costs. Costs incurred in identifying areas that may warrant examination and in examining specific areas that are considered to have prospects of containing oil and gas reserves, including costs of drilling exploratory wells and exploratory-type stratigraphic test wells. Exploration costs may be incurred both before acquiring the related property (sometimes referred to in part as prospecting costs) and after acquiring the property. Principal types of exploration costs, which include depreciation and applicable operating costs of support equipment and facilities and other costs of exploration activities, are:

(i) Costs of topographical, geographical and geophysical studies, rights of access to properties to conduct those studies, and salaries and other expenses of geologists, geophysical crews, and others conducting those studies. Collectively, these are sometimes referred to as geological and geophysical or G&G costs.

(ii) Costs of carrying and retaining undeveloped properties, such as delay rentals, ad valorem taxes on properties, legal costs for title defense, and the maintenance of land and lease records.

(iii) Dry hole contributions and bottom hole contributions.

(iv) Costs of drilling and equipping exploratory wells.

(v) Costs of drilling exploratory-type stratigraphic test wells.

(13) Exploratory well. An exploratory well is a well drilled to find a new field or to find a new reservoir in a field previously found to be productive of oil or gas in another reservoir. Generally, an exploratory well is any well that is not a development well, an extension well, a service well, or a stratigraphic test well as those items are defined in this section.

(14) Extension well. An extension well is a well drilled to extend the limits of a known reservoir.

(15) Field. An area consisting of a single reservoir or multiple reservoirs all grouped on or related to the same individual geological structural feature and/or stratigraphic condition. There may be two or more reservoirs in a field that are separated vertically by intervening impervious, strata, or laterally by local geologic barriers, or by both. Reservoirs that are associated by being in overlapping or adjacent fields may be treated as a single or common operational field. The geological terms structural feature and stratigraphic condition are intended to identify localized geological features as opposed to the broader terms of basins, trends, provinces, plays, areas-of-interest, etc.

(16) Oil and gas producing activities. (i) Oil and gas producing activities include:

(A) The search for crude oil, including condensate and natural gas liquids, or natural gas ("oil and gas") in their natural states and original locations;

(B) The acquisition of property rights or properties for the purpose of further exploration or for the purpose of removing the oil or gas from such properties;

(C) The construction, drilling, and production activities necessary to retrieve oil and gas from their natural reservoirs, including the acquisition, construction, installation, and maintenance of field gathering and storage systems, such as:

(1) Lifting the oil and gas to the surface; and

(2) Gathering, treating, and field processing (as in the case of processing gas to extract liquid hydrocarbons); and

65

(D) Extraction of saleable hydrocarbons, in the solid, liquid, or gaseous state, from oil sands, shale, coalbeds, or other nonrenewable natural resources which are intended to be upgraded into synthetic oil or gas, and activities undertaken with a view to such extraction.

Instruction 1 to paragraph (a)(16)(i): The oil and gas production function shall be regarded as ending at a "terminal point", which is the outlet valve on the lease or field storage tank. If unusual physical or operational circumstances exist, it may be appropriate to regard the terminal point for the production function as:

a. The first point at which oil, gas, or gas liquids, natural or synthetic, are delivered to a main pipeline, a common carrier, a refinery, or a marine terminal; and

b. In the case of natural resources that are intended to be upgraded into synthetic oil or gas, if those natural resources are delivered to a purchaser prior to upgrading, the first point at which the natural resources are delivered to a main pipeline, a common carrier, a refinery, a marine terminal, or a facility which upgrades such natural resources into synthetic oil or gas.

Instruction 2 to paragraph (a)(16)(i): For purposes of this paragraph (a)(16), the term saleable hydrocarbons means hydrocarbons that are saleable in the state in which the hydrocarbons are delivered.

(ii) Oil and gas producing activities do not include:

(A) Transporting, refining, or marketing oil and gas;

(B) Processing of produced oil, gas or natural resources that can be upgraded into synthetic oil or gas by a registrant that does not have the legal right to produce or a revenue interest in such production;

(C) Activities relating to the production of natural resources other than oil, gas, or natural resources from which synthetic oil and gas can be extracted; or

(D) Production of geothermal steam.

(17) Possible reserves. Possible reserves are those additional reserves that are less certain to be recovered than probable reserves.

(i) When deterministic methods are used, the total quantities ultimately recovered from a project have a low probability of exceeding proved plus probable plus possible reserves. When probabilistic methods are used, there should be at least a 10% probability that the total quantities ultimately recovered will equal or exceed the proved plus probable plus possible reserves estimates.

(ii) Possible reserves may be assigned to areas of a reservoir adjacent to probable reserves where data control and interpretations of available data are progressively less certain. Frequently, this will be in areas where geoscience and engineering data are unable to define clearly the area and vertical limits of commercial production from the reservoir by a defined project.

(iii) Possible reserves also include incremental quantities associated with a greater percentage recovery of the hydrocarbons in place than the recovery quantities assumed for probable reserves.

(iv) The proved plus probable and proved plus probable plus possible reserves estimates must be based on reasonable alternative technical and commercial interpretations within the reservoir or subject project that are clearly documented, including comparisons to results in successful similar projects.

(v) Possible reserves may be assigned where geoscience and engineering data identify directly adjacent portions of a reservoir within the same accumulation that may be separated from proved areas by faults with displacement less than formation thickness or other geological discontinuities and that have not been penetrated by a wellbore, and the registrant believes that such adjacent portions are in communication with the known (proved) reservoir. Possible reserves may be assigned to areas that are structurally higher or lower than the proved area if these areas are in communication with the proved reservoir.

(vi) Pursuant to paragraph (a)(22)(iii) of this section, where direct observation has defined a highest known oil (HKO) elevation and the potential exists for an associated gas cap, proved oil reserves should be assigned in the structurally higher portions of the reservoir above the HKO only if the higher contact can be established with reasonable certainty through reliable technology. Portions of the reservoir that do not meet this reasonable certainty criterion may be assigned as probable and possible oil or gas based on reservoir fluid properties and pressure gradient interpretations.

(18) Probable reserves. Probable reserves are those additional reserves that are less certain to be recovered than proved reserves but which, together with proved reserves, are as likely as not to be recovered.

(i) When deterministic methods are used, it is as likely as not that actual remaining quantities recovered will exceed the sum of estimated proved plus probable reserves. When probabilistic methods are used, there should be at least a 50% probability that the actual quantities recovered will equal or exceed the proved plus probable reserves estimates.

(ii) Probable reserves may be assigned to areas of a reservoir adjacent to proved reserves where data control or interpretations of available data are less certain, even if the interpreted reservoir continuity of structure or productivity does not meet the reasonable certainty criterion. Probable reserves may be assigned to areas that are structurally higher than the proved area if these areas are in communication with the proved reservoir.

(iii) Probable reserves estimates also include potential incremental quantities associated with a greater percentage recovery of the hydrocarbons in place than assumed for proved reserves.

(iv) See also guidelines in paragraphs (a)(17)(iv) and (a)(17)(vi) of this section.

(19) Probabilistic estimate. The method of estimation of reserves or resources is called probabilistic when the full range of values that could reasonably occur for each unknown parameter (from the geoscience and engineering data) is used to generate a full range of possible outcomes and their associated probabilities of occurrence.

(20) Production costs. (i) Costs incurred to operate and maintain wells and related equipment and facilities, including depreciation and applicable operating costs of support equipment and facilities and other costs of operating and maintaining those wells and related equipment and facilities. They become part of the cost of oil and gas produced. Examples of production costs (sometimes called lifting costs) are:

(A) Costs of labor to operate the wells and related equipment and facilities.

(B) Repairs and maintenance.

(C) Materials, supplies, and fuel consumed and supplies utilized in operating the wells and related equipment and facilities.

(D) Property taxes and insurance applicable to proved properties and wells and related equipment and facilities.

(E) Severance taxes.

(ii) Some support equipment or facilities may serve two or more oil and gas producing activities and may also serve transportation, refining, and marketing activities. To the extent that the support equipment and facilities are used in oil and gas producing activities, their depreciation and applicable operating costs become exploration, development or production costs, as appropriate. Depreciation, depletion, and amortization of capitalized acquisition, exploration, and development costs are not production costs but also become part of the cost of oil and gas produced along with production (lifting) costs identified above.

(21) Proved area. The part of a property to which proved reserves have been specifically attributed.

(22) Proved oil and gas reserves. Proved oil and gas reserves are those quantities of oil and gas, which, by analysis of geoscience and engineering data, can be estimated with reasonable certainty to be economically producible—from a given date forward, from known reservoirs, and under existing economic conditions, operating methods, and government regulations—prior to the time at which contracts providing the right to operate expire, unless evidence indicates that renewal is reasonably certain, regardless of whether deterministic or probabilistic methods are used for the estimation. The project to extract the hydrocarbons must have commenced or the operator must be reasonably certain that it will commence the project within a reasonable time.

(i) The area of the reservoir considered as proved includes:

(A) The area identified by drilling and limited by fluid contacts, if any, and

(B) Adjacent undrilled portions of the reservoir that can, with reasonable certainty, be judged to be continuous with it and to contain economically producible oil or gas on the basis of available geoscience and engineering data.

(ii) In the absence of data on fluid contacts, proved quantities in a reservoir are limited by the lowest known hydrocarbons (LKH) as seen in a well penetration unless geoscience, engineering, or performance data and reliable technology establishes a lower contact with reasonable certainty.

(iii) Where direct observation from well penetrations has defined a highest known oil (HKO) elevation and the potential exists for an associated gas cap, proved oil reserves may be assigned in the structurally higher portions of the reservoir only if geoscience, engineering, or performance data and reliable technology establish the higher contact with reasonable certainty.

(iv) Reserves which can be produced economically through application of improved recovery techniques (including, but not limited to, fluid injection) are included in the proved classification when:

(A) Successful testing by a pilot project in an area of the reservoir with properties no more favorable than in the reservoir as a whole, the operation of an installed program in the reservoir or an analogous reservoir, or other evidence using reliable technology establishes the reasonable certainty of the engineering analysis on which the project or program was based; and

(B) The project has been approved for development by all necessary parties and entities, including governmental entities.

(v) Existing economic conditions include prices and costs at which economic producibility from a reservoir is to be determined. The price shall be the average price during the 12-month period prior to the ending date of the period covered by the report, determined as an unweighted arithmetic average of the first-day-of-the-month price for each month within such period, unless prices are defined by contractual arrangements, excluding escalations based upon future conditions.

(23) Proved properties. Properties with proved reserves.

(24) Reasonable certainty. If deterministic methods are used, reasonable certainty means a high degree of confidence that the quantities will be recovered. If probabilistic methods are used, there should be at least a 90% probability that the quantities actually recovered will equal or exceed the estimate. A high degree of confidence exists if the quantity is much more likely to be achieved than not, and, as changes due to increased availability of geoscience (geological, geophysical, and geochemical), engineering, and economic data are made to estimated ultimate recovery (EUR) with time, reasonably certain EUR is much more likely to increase or remain constant than to decrease.

(25) Reliable technology. Reliable technology is a grouping of one or more technologies (including computational methods) that has been field tested and has been demonstrated to provide reasonably certain results with consistency and repeatability in the formation being evaluated or in an analogous formation.

(26) Reserves. Reserves are estimated remaining quantities of oil and gas and related substances anticipated to be economically producible, as of a given date, by application of development projects to known accumulations. In addition, there must exist, or there must be a reasonable expectation that there will exist, the legal right to produce or a revenue interest in the production, installed means of delivering oil and gas or related substances to market, and all permits and financing required to implement the project.

Note to paragraph (a)(26): Reserves should not be assigned to adjacent reservoirs isolated by major, potentially sealing, faults until those reservoirs are penetrated and evaluated as economically producible. Reserves should not be assigned to areas that are clearly separated from a known accumulation by a non-productive reservoir (i.e., absence of reservoir, structurally low reservoir, or negative test results). Such areas may contain prospective resources (i.e., potentially recoverable resources from undiscovered accumulations).

(27) Reservoir. A porous and permeable underground formation containing a natural accumulation of producible oil and/or gas that is confined by impermeable rock or water barriers and is individual and separate from other reservoirs.

(28) Resources. Resources are quantities of oil and gas estimated to exist in naturally occurring accumulations. A portion of the resources may be estimated to be recoverable, and another portion may be considered to be unrecoverable. Resources include both discovered and undiscovered accumulations.

(29) Service well. A well drilled or completed for the purpose of supporting production in an existing field. Specific purposes of service wells include gas injection, water injection, steam injection, air injection, salt-water disposal, water supply for injection, observation, or injection for in-situ combustion.

(30) Stratigraphic test well. A stratigraphic test well is a drilling effort, geologically directed, to obtain information pertaining to a specific geologic condition. Such wells customarily are drilled without the intent of being completed for hydrocarbon production. The classification also includes tests identified as core tests and all types of expendable holes related to hydrocarbon exploration. Stratigraphic tests are classified as "exploratory type" if not drilled in a known area or "development type" if drilled in a known area.

(31) Undeveloped oil and gas reserves. Undeveloped oil and gas reserves are reserves of any category that are expected to be recovered from new wells on undrilled acreage, or from existing wells where a relatively major expenditure is required for recompletion.

(i) Reserves on undrilled acreage shall be limited to those directly offsetting development spacing areas that are reasonably certain of production when drilled, unless evidence using reliable technology exists that establishes reasonable certainty of economic producibility at greater distances.

(ii) Undrilled locations can be classified as having undeveloped reserves only if a development plan has been adopted indicating that they are scheduled to be drilled within five years, unless the specific circumstances, justify a longer time.

(iii) Under no circumstances shall estimates for undeveloped reserves be attributable to any acreage for which an application of fluid injection or other improved recovery technique is contemplated, unless such techniques have been proved effective by actual projects in the same reservoir or an analogous reservoir, as defined in paragraph (a)(2) of this section, or by other evidence using reliable technology establishing reasonable certainty.

(32) Unproved properties. Properties with no proved reserves.

Successful Efforts Method
(b) A reporting entity that follows the successful efforts method shall comply with the accounting and financial reporting disclosure requirements of FASB ASC Topic 932, Extractive Activities—Oil and Gas.

Full Cost Method
(c) Application of the full cost method of accounting. A reporting entity that follows the full cost method shall apply that method to all of its operations and to the operations of its subsidiaries, as follows:

(1) Determination of cost centers. Cost centers shall be established on a country-by-country basis.

(2) Costs to be capitalized. All costs associated with property acquisition, exploration, and development activities (as defined in paragraph (a) of this section) shall be capitalized within the appropriate cost center. Any internal costs that are capitalized shall be limited to those costs that can be directly identified with acquisition, exploration, and development activities undertaken by the reporting entity for its own account, and shall not include any costs related to production, general corporate overhead, or similar activities.

(3) Amortization of capitalized costs. Capitalized costs within a cost center shall be amortized on the unit-of-production basis using proved oil and gas reserves, as follows:

(i) Costs to be amortized shall include (A) all capitalized costs, less accumulated amortization, other than the cost of properties described in paragraph (ii) below; (B) the estimated future expenditures (based on current costs) to be incurred in developing proved reserves; and (C) estimated dismantlement and abandonment costs, net of estimated salvage values.

(ii) The cost of investments in unproved properties and major development projects may be excluded from capitalized costs to be amortized, subject to the following:

(A) All costs directly associated with the acquisition and evaluation of unproved properties may be excluded from the amortization computation until it is determined whether or not proved reserves can be assigned to the properties, subject to the following conditions:

(1) Until such a determination is made, the properties shall be assessed at least annually to ascertain whether impairment has occurred. Unevaluated properties whose costs are individually significant shall be assessed individually. Where it is not practicable to individually assess the amount of impairment of properties for which costs are not individually significant, such properties may be grouped for purposes of assessing impairment. Impairment may be estimated by applying factors based on historical experience and other data such as primary lease terms of the properties, average holding periods of unproved properties, and geographic and geologic data to groupings of individually insignificant properties and projects. The amount of impairment assessed under either of these methods shall be added to the costs to be amortized.

(2) The costs of drilling exploratory dry holes shall be included in the amortization base immediately upon determination that the well is dry.

(3) If geological and geophysical costs cannot be directly associated with specific unevaluated properties, they shall be included in the amortization base as incurred. Upon complete evaluation of a property, the total remaining excluded cost (net of any impairment) shall be included in the full cost amortization base.

(B) Certain costs may be excluded from amortization when incurred in connection with major development projects expected to entail significant costs to ascertain the quantities of proved reserves attributable to the properties under development (e.g., the installation of an offshore drilling platform from which development wells are to be drilled, the installation of improved recovery programs, and similar major projects undertaken in the expectation of significant additions to proved reserves). The amounts which may be excluded are applicable portions of (1) the costs that relate to the major development project and have not previously been included in the amortization base, and (2) the estimated future expenditures associated with the development project. The excluded portion of any common costs associated with the development project should be based, as is most appropriate in the circumstances, on a comparison of either (i) existing proved reserves to total proved reserves expected to be established upon completion of the project, or (ii) the number of wells to which proved reserves have been assigned and total number of wells expected to be drilled. Such costs may be excluded from costs to be amortized until the earlier determination of whether additional reserves are proved or impairment occurs.

(C) Excluded costs and the proved reserves related to such costs shall be transferred into the amortization base on an ongoing (well-by-well or property-by-property) basis as the project is evaluated and proved reserves established or impairment determined. Once proved reserves are established, there is no further justification for continued exclusion from the full cost amortization base even if other factors prevent immediate production or marketing.

(iii) Amortization shall be computed on the basis of physical units, with oil and gas converted to a common unit of measure on the basis of their approximate relative energy content, unless economic circumstances (related to the effects of regulated prices) indicate that use of units of revenue is a more appropriate basis of computing amortization. In the latter case, amortization shall be computed on the basis of current gross revenues (excluding royalty payments and net profits disbursements) from production in relation to future gross revenues, based on current prices (including consideration of changes in existing prices provided only by contractual arrangements), from estimated production of proved oil and gas reserves. The effect of a significant price increase during the year on estimated future gross revenues shall be reflected in the amortization provision only for the period after the price increase occurs.

(iv) In some cases it may be more appropriate to depreciate natural gas cycling and processing plants by a method other than the unit-of-production method.

(v) Amortization computations shall be made on a consolidated basis, including investees accounted for on a proportionate consolidation basis. Investees accounted for on the equity method shall be treated separately.

(4) Limitation on capitalized costs. (i) For each cost center, capitalized costs, less accumulated amortization and related deferred income taxes, shall not exceed an amount (the cost center ceiling) equal to the sum of:

(A) The present value of estimated future net revenues computed by applying current prices of oil and gas reserves (with consideration of price changes only to the extent provided by contractual arrangements) to estimated future production of proved oil and gas reserves as of the date of the latest balance sheet presented, less estimated future expenditures (based on current costs) to be incurred in developing and producing the proved reserves computed using a discount factor of ten percent and assuming continuation of existing economic conditions; plus

(B) the cost of properties not being amortized pursuant to paragraph (i)(3)(ii) of this section; plus

(C) the lower of cost or estimated fair value of unproven properties included in the costs being amortized; less

(D) income tax effects related to differences between the book and tax basis of the properties referred to in paragraphs (i)(4)(i) (B) and (C) of this section.

(ii) If unamortized costs capitalized within a cost center, less related deferred income taxes, exceed the cost center ceiling, the excess shall be charged to expense and separately disclosed during the period in which the excess occurs. Amounts thus required to be written off shall not be reinstated for any subsequent increase in the cost center ceiling.

(5) Production costs. All costs relating to production activities, including workover costs incurred solely to maintain or increase levels of production from an existing completion interval, shall be charged to expense as incurred.

(6) Other transactions. The provisions of paragraph (h) of this section, "Mineral property conveyances and related transactions if the successful efforts method of accounting is followed," shall apply also to those reporting entities following the full cost method except as follows:

(i) Sales and abandonments of oil and gas properties. Sales of oil and gas properties, whether or not being amortized currently, shall be accounted for as adjustments of capitalized costs, with no gain or loss recognized, unless such adjustments would significantly alter the relationship between capitalized costs and proved reserves of oil and gas attributable to a cost center. For instance, a significant alteration would not ordinarily be expected to occur for sales involving less than 25 percent of the reserve quantities of a given cost center. If gain or loss is recognized on such a sale, total capitalization costs within the cost center shall be allocated between the reserves sold and reserves retained on the same basis used to compute amortization, unless there are substantial economic differences between the properties sold and those retained, in which case capitalized costs shall be allocated on the basis of the relative fair values of the properties. Abandonments of oil and gas properties shall be accounted for as adjustments of capitalized costs; that is, the cost of abandoned properties shall be charged to the full cost center and amortized (subject to the limitation on capitalized costs in paragraph (b) of this section).

(ii) Purchases of reserves. Purchases of oil and gas reserves in place ordinarily shall be accounted for as additional capitalized costs within the applicable cost center; however, significant purchases of production payments or properties with lives substantially shorter than the composite productive life of the cost center shall be accounted for separately.

(iii) Partnerships, joint ventures and drilling arrangements. (A) Except as provided in paragraph (i)(6)(i) of this section, all consideration received from sales or transfers of properties in connection with partnerships, joint venture operations, or various other forms of drilling arrangements involving oil and gas exploration and development activities (e.g., carried interest, turnkey wells, management fees, etc.) shall be credited to the full cost account, except to the extent of amounts that represent reimbursement of organization, offering, general and administrative expenses, etc., that are identifiable with the transaction, if such amounts are currently incurred and charged to expense.

(B) Where a registrant organizes and manages a limited partnership involved only in the purchase of proved developed properties and subsequent distribution of income from such properties, management fee income may be recognized provided the properties involved do not require aggregate development expenditures in connection with production of existing proved reserves in excess of 10% of the partnership's recorded cost of such properties. Any income not recognized as a result of this limitation would be credited to the full cost account and recognized through a lower amortization provision as reserves are produced.

(iv) Other services. No income shall be recognized in connection with contractual services performed (e.g. drilling, well service, or equipment supply services, etc.) in connection with properties in which the registrant or an affiliate (as defined in §210.1-02(b)) holds an ownership or other economic interest, except as follows:

(A) Where the registrant acquires an interest in the properties in connection with the service contract, income may be recognized to the extent the cash consideration received exceeds the related contract costs plus the registrant's share of costs incurred and estimated to be incurred in connection with the properties. Ownership interests acquired within one year of the date of such a contract are considered to be acquired in connection with the service for purposes of applying this rule. The amount of any guarantees or similar arrangements undertaken as part of this contract should be considered as part of the costs related to the properties for purposes of applying this rule.

(B) Where the registrant acquired an interest in the properties at least one year before the date of the service contract through transactions unrelated to the service contract, and that interest is unaffected by the service contract, income from such contract may be recognized subject to the general provisions for elimination of inter-company profit under generally accepted accounting principles.

(C) Notwithstanding the provisions of paragraphs (i)(6)(iv) (A) and (B) of this section, no income may be recognized for contractual services performed on behalf of investors in oil and gas producing activities managed by the registrant or an affiliate. Furthermore, no income may be recognized for contractual services to the extent that the consideration received for such services represents an interest in the underlying property.

(D) Any income not recognized as a result of these rules would be credited to the full cost account and recognized through a lower amortization provision as reserves are produced.

(7) Disclosures. Reporting entities that follow the full cost method of accounting shall disclose all of the information required by paragraph (k) of this section, with each cost center considered as a separate geographic area, except that reasonable groupings may be made of cost centers that are not significant in the aggregate. In addition:

(i) For each cost center for each year that an income statement is required, disclose the total amount of amortization expense (per equivalent physical unit of production if amortization is computed on the basis of physical units or per dollar of gross revenue from production if amortization is computed on the basis of gross revenue).

(ii) State separately on the face of the balance sheet the aggregate of the capitalized costs of unproved properties and major development projects that are excluded, in accordance with paragraph (i)(3) of this section, from the capitalized costs being amortized. Provide a description in the notes to the financial statements of the current status of the significant properties or projects involved, including the anticipated timing of the inclusion of the costs in the amortization computation. Present a table that shows, by category of cost, (A) the total costs excluded as of the most recent fiscal year; and (B) the amounts of such excluded costs, incurred (1) in each of the three most recent fiscal years and (2) in the aggregate for any earlier fiscal years in which the costs were incurred. Categories of cost to be disclosed include acquisition costs, exploration costs, development costs in the case of significant development projects and capitalized interest.

(8) For purposes of this paragraph (c), the term "current price" shall mean the average price during the 12-month period prior to the ending date of the period covered by the report, determined as an unweighted arithmetic average of the first-day-of-the-month price for each month within such period, unless prices are defined by contractual arrangements, excluding escalations based upon future conditions.

Income Taxes

(d) Income taxes. Comprehensive interperiod income tax allocation by a method which complies with generally accepted accounting principles shall be followed for intangible drilling and development costs and other costs incurred that enter into the determination of taxable income and pretax accounting income in different periods.

[43 FR 60405, Dec. 27, 1978, as amended at 43 FR 60417, Dec. 27, 1978; 44 FR 57036, 57038, Oct. 9, 1979; 45 FR 27749, Apr. 24, 1980. Redesignated and amended at 45 FR 63669, Sept. 25, 1980; 47 FR 57913, Dec. 29, 1982; 48 FR 44200, Sept. 28, 1983; 49 FR 18473, May 1, 1984; 57 FR 45293, Oct. 1, 1992; 61 FR 30401, June 14, 1996; 74 FR 2190, Jan. 14, 2009; 76 FR 50119, Aug. 12, 2011]

Commercial and Industrial Companies

§210.5-01   Application of §§210.5-01 to 210.5-04.
Sections 210.5-01 to 210.5-04 shall be applicable to financial statements filed for all persons except—

(a) Registered investment companies (see §§210.6-01 to 210.6-10).

(b) Employee stock purchase, savings and similar plans (see §§210.6A-01 to 210.6A-05).

(c) Insurance companies (see §§210.7-01 to 210.7-05).

(d) Bank holding companies and banks (see §§210.9-01 to 210.9-07).

(e) Brokers and dealers when filing Form X-17A-5 [249.617] (see §§240.17a-5 and 240.17a-10 under the Securities Exchange Act of 1934).

[50 FR 49533, Dec. 3, 1985]

§210.5-02   Balance sheets.
The purpose of this rule is to indicate the various line items and certain additional disclosures which, if applicable, and except as otherwise permitted by the Commission, should appear on the face of the balance sheets or related notes filed for the persons to whom this article pertains (see §210.4-01(a)).

Assets and Other Debits
Current Assets, when appropriate
[See §210.4-05]
1. Cash and cash items. Separate disclosure shall be made of the cash and cash items which are restricted as to withdrawal or usage. The provisions of any restrictions shall be described in a note to the financial statements. Restrictions may include legally restricted deposits held as compensating balances against short-term borrowing arrangements, contracts entered into with others, or company statements of intention with regard to particular deposits; however, time deposits and short-term certificates of deposit are not generally included in legally restricted deposits. In cases where compensating balance arrangements exist but are not agreements which legally restrict the use of cash amounts shown on the balance sheet, describe in the notes to the financial statements these arrangements and the amount involved, if determinable, for the most recent audited balance sheet required and for any subsequent unaudited balance sheet required in the notes to the financial statements. Compensating balances that are maintained under an agreement to assure future credit availability shall be disclosed in the notes to the financial statements along with the amount and terms of such agreement.

2. Marketable securities. The accounting and disclosure requirements for current marketable equity securities are specified by generally accepted accounting principles. With respect to all other current marketable securities, state, parenthetically or otherwise, the basis of determining the aggregate amount shown in the balance sheet, along with the alternatives of the aggregate cost or the aggregate market value at the balance sheet date.

3. Accounts and notes receivable. (a) State separately amounts receivable from (1) customers (trade); (2) related parties (see §210.4-08(k)); (3) underwriters, promoters, and employees (other than related parties) which arose in other than the ordinary course of business; and (4) others.

(b) If the aggregate amount of notes receivable exceeds 10 percent of the aggregate amount of receivables, the above information shall be set forth separately, in the balance sheet or in a note thereto, for accounts receivable and notes receivable.

(c) If receivables include amounts due under long-term contracts (see §210.5-02.6(d)), state separately in the balance sheet or in a note to the financial statements the following amounts:

(1) Balances billed but not paid by customers under retainage provisions in contracts.

(2) Amounts representing the recognized sales value of performance and such amounts that had not been billed and were not billable to customers at the date of the balance sheet. Include a general description of the prerequisites for billing.

(3) Billed or unbilled amounts representing claims or other similar items subject to uncertainty concerning their determination or ultimate realization. Include a description of the nature and status of the principal items comprising such amount.

(4) With respect to (1) through (3) above, also state the amounts included in each item which are expected to be collected after one year. Also state, by year, if practicable, when the amounts of retainage (see (1) above) are expected to be collected.

4. Allowances for doubtful accounts and notes receivable. The amount is to be set forth separately in the balance sheet or in a note thereto.

5. Unearned income.

6. Inventories. (a) State separately in the balance sheet or in a note thereto, if practicable, the amounts of major classes of inventory such as: (1) Finished goods; (2) inventoried costs relating to long-term contracts or programs (see (d) below and §210.4-05); (3) work in process (see §210.4-05); (4) raw materials; and (5) supplies. If the method of calculating a LIFO inventory does not allow for the practical determination of amounts assigned to major classes of inventory, the amounts of those classes may be stated under cost flow assumptions other that LIFO with the excess of such total amount over the aggregate LIFO amount shown as a deduction to arrive at the amount of the LIFO inventory.

(b) The basis of determining the amounts shall be stated.

If cost is used to determine any portion of the inventory amounts, the description of this method shall include the nature of the cost elements included in inventory. Elements of cost include, among other items, retained costs representing the excess of manufacturing or production costs over the amounts charged to cost of sales or delivered or in-process units, initial tooling or other deferred startup costs, or general and administrative costs.

The method by which amounts are removed from inventory (e.g., average cost, first-in, first-out, last-in, first-out, estimated average cost per unit) shall be described. If the estimated average cost per unit is used as a basis to determine amounts removed from inventory under a total program or similar basis of accounting, the principal assumptions (including, where meaningful, the aggregate number of units expected to be delivered under the program, the number of units delivered to date and the number of units on order) shall be disclosed.

If any general and administrative costs are charged to inventory, state in a note to the financial statements the aggregate amount of the general and administrative costs incurred in each period and the actual or estimated amount remaining in inventory at the date of each balance sheet.

(c) If the LIFO inventory method is used, the excess of replacement or current cost over stated LIFO value shall, if material, be stated parenthetically or in a note to the financial statements.

(d) For purposes of §§210.5-02.3 and 210.5-02.6, long-term contracts or programs include (1) all contracts or programs for which gross profits are recognized on a percentage-of-completion method of accounting or any variant thereof (e.g., delivered unit, cost to cost, physical completion), and (2) any contracts or programs accounted for on a completed contract basis of accounting where, in either case, the contracts or programs have associated with them material amounts of inventories or unbilled receivables and where such contracts or programs have been or are expected to be performed over a period of more than twelve months. Contracts or programs of shorter duration may also be included, if deemed appropriate.

For all long-term contracts or programs, the following information, if applicable, shall be stated in a note to the financial statements:

(i) The aggregate amount of manufacturing or production costs and any related deferred costs (e.g., initial tooling costs) which exceeds the aggregate estimated cost of all in-process and delivered units on the basis of the estimated average cost of all units expected to be produced under long-term contracts and programs not yet complete, as well as that portion of such amount which would not be absorbed in cost of sales based on existing firm orders at the latest balance sheet date. In addition, if practicable, disclose the amount of deferred costs by type of cost (e.g., initial tooling, deferred production, etc.).

(ii) The aggregate amount representing claims or other similar items subject to uncertainty concerning their determination or ultimate realization, and include a description of the nature and status of the principal items comprising such aggregate amount.

(iii) The amount of progress payments netted against inventory at the date of the balance sheet.

7. Prepaid expenses.

8. Other current assets. State separately, in the balance sheet or in a note thereto, any amounts in excess of five percent of total current assets.

9. Total current assets, when appropriate.

10. Securities of related parties. (See §210.4-08(k).)

11. Indebtedness of related parties—not current. (See §210.4-08(k).)

12. Other investments. The accounting and disclosure requirements for non-current marketable equity securities are specified by generally accepted accounting principles. With respect to other security investments and any other investment, state, parenthetically or otherwise, the basis of determining the aggregate amounts shown in the balance sheet, along with the alternate of the aggregate cost or aggregate market value at the balance sheet date.

13. Property, plant and equipment.

(a) State the basis of determining the amounts.

(b) Tangible and intangible utility plant of a public utility company shall be segregated so as to show separately the original cost, plant acquisition adjustments, and plant adjustments, as required by the system of accounts prescribed by the applicable regulatory authorities. This rule shall not be applicable in respect to companies which are not required to make such a classification.

14. Accumulated depreciation, depletion, and amortization of property, plant and equipment. The amount is to be set forth separately in the balance sheet or in a note thereto.

15. Intangible assets. State separately each class of such assets which is in excess of five percent of the total assets, along with the basis of determining the respective amounts. Any significant addition or deletion shall be explained in a note.

16. Accumulated depreciation and amortization of intangible assets. The amount is to be set forth separately in the balance sheet or in a note thereto.

17. Other assets. State separately, in the balance sheet or in a note thereto, any other item not properly classed in one of the preceding asset captions which is in excess of five percent to total assets. Any significant addition or deletion should be explained in a note. With respect to any significant deferred charge, state the policy for deferral and amortization.

18. Total assets.

Liabilities and Stockholders' Equity
Current Liabilities, When Appropriate (See §210.4-05)
19. Accounts and notes payable. (a) State separately amounts payable to (1) banks for borrowings; (2) factors or other financial institutions for borrowings; (3) holders of commercial paper; (4) trade creditors; (5) related parties (see §210.4-08(k)); (6) underwriters, promoters, and employees (other than related parties); and (7) others. Amounts applicable to (1), (2) and (3) may be stated separately in the balance sheet or in a note thereto.

(b) The amount and terms (including commitment fees and the conditions under which lines may be withdrawn) of unused lines of credit for short-term financing shall be disclosed, if significant, in the notes to the financial statements. The weighted average interest rate on short term borrowings outstanding as of the date of each balance sheet presented shall be furnished in a note. The amount of these lines of credit which support a commercial paper borrowing arrangement or similar arrangements shall be separately identified.

20. Other current liabilities. State separately, in the balance sheet or in a note thereto, any item in excess of 5 percent of total current liabilities. Such items may include, but are not limited to, accrued payrolls, accrued interest, taxes, indicating the current portion of deferred income taxes, and the current portion of long-term debt. Remaining items may be shown in one amount.

21. Total current liabilities, when appropriate.

Long-Term Debt
22. Bonds, mortgages and other long-term debt, including capitalized leases. (a) State separately, in the balance sheet or in a note thereto, each issue or type of obligation and such information as will indicate (see §210.4-06):

(1) The general character of each type of debt including the rate of interest; (2) the date of maturity, or, if maturing serially, a brief indication of the serial maturities, such as "maturing serially from 1980 to 1990"; (3) if the payment of principal or interest is contingent, an appropriate indication of such contingency; (4) a brief indication of priority; and (5) if convertible, the basis. For amounts owed to related parties, see §210.4-08(k).

(b) The amount and terms (including commitment fees and the conditions under which commitments may be withdrawn) of unused commitments for long-term financing arrangements that would be disclosed under this rule if used shall be disclosed in the notes to the financial statements if significant.

23. Indebtedness to related parties—noncurrent. Include under this caption indebtedness to related parties as required under §210.4-08(k).

24. Other liabilities. State separately, in the balance sheet or in a note thereto, any item not properly classified in one of the preceding liability captions which is in excess of 5 percent of total liabilities.

25. Commitments and contingent liabilities.

26. Deferred credits. State separately in the balance sheet amounts for (a) deferred income taxes, (b) deferred tax credits, and (c) material items of deferred income.

Redeemable Preferred Stocks
27. Preferred stocks subject to mandatory redemption requirements or whose redemption is outside the control of the issuer. (a) Include under this caption amounts applicable to any class of stock which has any of the following characteristics: (1) it is redeemable at a fixed or determinable price on a fixed or determinable date or dates, whether by operation of a sinking fund or otherwise; (2) it is redeemable at the option of the holder; or (3) it has conditions for redemption which are not solely within the control of the issuer, such as stocks which must be redeemed out of future earnings. Amounts attributable to preferred stock which is not redeemable or is redeemable solely at the option of the issuer shall be included under §210.5-02.28 unless it meets one or more of the above criteria.

(b) State on the face of the balance sheet the title of each issue, the carrying amount, and redemption amount. (If there is more than one issue, these amounts may be aggregated on the face of the balance sheet and details concerning each issue may be presented in the note required by paragraph (c) below.) Show also the dollar amount of any shares subscribed but unissued, and show the deduction of subscriptions receivable therefrom. If the carrying value is different from the redemption amount, describe the accounting treatment for such difference in the note required by paragraph (c) below. Also state in this note or on the face of the balance sheet, for each issue, the number of shares authorized and the number of shares issued or outstanding, as appropriate (See §210.4-07).

(c) State in a separate note captioned "Redeemable Preferred Stocks" (1) a general description of each issue, including its redemption features (e.g. sinking fund, at option of holders, out of future earnings) and the rights, if any, of holders in the event of default, including the effect, if any, on junior securities in the event a required dividend, sinking fund, or other redemption payment(s) is not made; (2) the combined aggregate amount of redemption requirements for all issues each year for the five years following the date of the latest balance sheet; and (3) the changes in each issue for each period for which an income statement is required to be filed. (See also §210.4-08(d).)

(d) Securities reported under this caption are not to be included under a general heading "stockholders' equity" or combined in a total with items described in captions 29, 30 or 31 which follow.

Non-Redeemable Preferred Stocks

28. Preferred stocks which are not redeemable or are redeemable solely at the option of the issuer. State on the face of the balance sheet, or if more than one issue is outstanding state in a note, the title of each issue and the dollar amount thereof. Show also the dollar amount of any shares subscribed but unissued, and show the deduction of subscriptions receivable therefrom. State on the face of the balance sheet or in a note, for each issue, the number of shares authorized and the number of shares issued or outstanding, as appropriate (see §210.4-07). Show in a note or separate statement the changes in each class of preferred shares reported under this caption for each period for which an income statement is required to be filed. (See also §210.4-08(d).)

Common Stocks

29. Common stocks. For each class of common shares state, on the face of the balance sheet, the number of shares issued or outstanding, as appropriate (see §210.4-07), and the dollar amount thereof. If convertible, this fact should be indicated on the face of the balance sheet. For each class of common shares state, on the face of the balance sheet or in a note, the title of the issue, the number of shares authorized, and, if convertible, the basis of conversion (see also §210.4-08(d)). Show also the dollar amount of any common shares subscribed but unissued, and show the deduction of subscriptions receivable therefrom. Show in a note or statement the changes in each class of common shares for each period for which an income statement is required to be filed.

Other Stockholders' Equity

30. Other stockholders' equity. (a) Separate captions shall be shown for (1) additional paid-in capital, (2) other additional capital and (3) retained earnings (i) appropriated and (ii) unappropriated. (See §210.4-08(e).) Additional paid-in capital and other additional capital may be combined with the stock caption to which it applies, if appropriate.

(b) For a period of at least 10 years subsequent to the effective date of a quasi-reorganization, any description of retained earnings shall indicate the point in time from which the new retained earnings dates and for a period of at least three years shall indicate, on the face of the balance sheet, the total amount of the deficit eliminated.

Noncontrolling Interests

31. Noncontrolling interests in consolidated subsidiaries. State separately in a note the amounts represented by preferred stock and the applicable dividend requirements if the preferred stock is material in relation to the consolidated equity.

32. Total liabilities and equity.

[45 FR 63671, Sept. 25, 1980, as amended at 46 FR 43412, Aug. 28, 1981; 47 FR 29837, July 9, 1982; 50 FR 25215, June 18, 1985; 50 FR 49533, Dec. 3, 1985; 59 FR 65636, Dec. 20, 1994; 74 FR 18615, Apr. 23, 2009]

§210.5-03 Income statements.

(a) The purpose of this rule is to indicate the various line items which, if applicable, and except as otherwise permitted by the Commission, should appear on the face of the income statements filed for the persons to whom this article pertains (see §210.4-01(a)).

(b) If income is derived from more than one of the subcaptions described under §210.5-03.1, each class which is not more than 10 percent of the sum of the items may be combined with another class. If these items are combined, related costs and expenses as described under §210.5-03.2 shall be combined in the same manner.

1. Net sales and gross revenues. State separately:

(a) Net sales of tangible products (gross sales less discounts, returns and allowances), (b) operating revenues of public utilities or others; (c) income from rentals; (d) revenues from services; and (e) other revenues. Amounts earned from transactions with related parties shall be disclosed as required under §210.4-08(k). A public utility company using a uniform system of accounts or a form for annual report prescribed by federal or state authorities, or a similar system or report, shall follow the general segregation of operating revenues and operating expenses reported under §210.5-03.2 prescribed by such system or report. If the total of sales and revenues reported under this caption includes excise taxes in an amount equal to 1 percent or more of such total, the amount of such excise taxes shall be shown on the face of the statement parenthetically or othewise.

2. Costs and expenses applicable to sales and revenues.

State separately the amount of (a) cost of tangible goods sold, (b) operating expenses of public utilities or others, (c) expenses applicable to rental income, (d) cost of services, and (e) expenses applicable to other revenues. Merchandising organizations, both wholesale and retail, may include occupancy and buying costs under caption 2(a). Amounts of costs and expenses incurred from transactions with related parties shall be disclosed as required under §210.4-08(k).

3. Other operating costs and expenses. State separately any material amounts not included under caption 2 above.

4. Selling, general and administrative expenses.

5. Provision for doubtful accounts and notes.

6. Other general expenses. Include items not normally included in caption 4 above. State separately any material item.

7. Non-operating income.

State separately in the income statement or in a note thereto amounts earned from (a) dividends, (b) interest on securities, (c) profits on securities (net of losses), and (d) miscellaneous other income. Amounts earned from transactions in securities of related parties shall be disclosed as required under §210.4-08(k). Material amounts included under miscellaneous other income shall be separately stated in the income statement or in a note thereto, indicating clearly the nature of the transactions out of which the items arose.

8. Interest and amortization of debt discount and expense.

9. Non-operating expenses.

State separately in the income statement or in a note thereto amounts of (a) losses on securities (net of profits) and (b) miscellaneous income deductions. Material amounts included under miscellaneous income deductions shall be separately stated in the income statement or in a note thereto, indicating clearly the nature of the transactions out of which the items arose.

10. Income or loss before income tax expense and appropriate items below.

11. Income tax expense. Include under this caption only taxes based on income (see §210.4-08(h)).

12. Equity in earnings of unconsolidated subsidiaries and 50 percent or less owned persons. State, parenthetically or in a note, the amount of dividends received from such persons. If justified by the circumstances, this item may be presented in a different position and a different manner (see §210.4-01(a)).

13. Income or loss from continuing operations.

14. Discontinued operations.

15. Income or loss before extraordinary items and cumulative effects of changes in accounting principles.

16. Extraordinary items, less applicable tax.

17. Cumulative effects of changes in accounting principles.

18. Net income or loss.

19. Net income attributable to the noncontrolling interest.

20. Net income attributable to the controlling interest.

21. Earnings per share data.

[45 FR 63671, Sept. 25, 1980, as amended at 45 FR 76977, Nov. 21, 1980; 50 FR 25215, June 18, 1985; 74 FR 18615, Apr. 23, 2009]

§210.5-04   What schedules are to be filed.
(a) Except as expressly provided otherwise in the applicable form:

(1) The schedules specified below in this Section as Schedules II and III shall be filed as of the date of the most recent audited balanced sheet for each person or group.

(2) Schedule II shall be filed for each period for which an audited income statement is required to be filed for each person or group.

(3) Schedules I and IV shall be filed as of the date and for periods specified in the schedule.

(b) When information is required in schedules for both the registrant and the registrant and its subsidiaries consolidated it may be presented in the form of a single schedule: Provided, That items pertaining to the registrant are separately shown and that such single schedule affords a properly summarized presentation of the facts. If the information required by any schedule (including the notes thereto) may be shown in the related financial statement or in a note thereto without making such statement unclear or confusing, that procedure may be followed and the schedule omitted.

(c) The schedules shall be examined by the independent accountant if the related financial statements are so examined.

Schedule I—Condensed financial information of registrant. The schedule prescribed by §210.12-04 shall be filed when the restricted net assets (§210.4-08(e)(3)) of consolidated subsidiaries exceed 25 percent of consolidated net assets as of the end of the most recently completed fiscal year. For purposes of the above test, restricted net assets of consolidated subsidiaries shall mean that amount of the registrant's proportionate share of net assets of consolidated subsidiaries (after intercompany eliminations) which as of the end of the most recent fiscal year may not be transferred to the parent company by subsidiaries in the form of loans, advances or cash dividends without the consent of a third party (i.e., lender, regulatory agency, foreign government, etc.). Where restrictions on the amount of funds which may be loaned or advanced differ from the amount restricted as to transfer in the form of cash dividends, the amount least restrictive to the subsidiary shall be used. Redeemable preferred stocks (§210.5-02.27) and noncontrolling interests shall be deducted in computing net assets for purposes of this test.

Schedule II—Valuation and qualifying accounts. The schedule prescribed by §210.12-09 shall be filed in support of valuation and qualifying accounts included in each balance sheet but not included in Schedule VI. (See §210.4-02.)

Schedule III—Real estate and accumulated depreciation. The schedule prescribed by §210.12-28 shall be filed for real estate (and the related accumulated depreciation) held by persons a substantial portion of whose business is that of acquiring and holding for investment real estate or interests in real estate, or interests in other persons a substantial portion of whose business is that of acquiring and holding real estate or interests in real estate for investment. Real estate used in the business shall be excluded from the schedule.

Schedule IV—Mortgage loans on real estate. The schedule prescribed by §210.12-29 shall be filed by persons specified under Schedule XI for investments in mortgage loans on real estate.

Schedule V—Supplemental Information Concerning Property-casualty Insurance Operations. The schedule prescribed by §210.12-18 shall be filed when a registrant, its subsidiaries or 50%-or-less-owned equity basis investees, have liabilities for property-casualty ("P/C") insurance claims. The required information shall be presented as of the same dates and for the same periods for which the information is reflected in the audited consolidated financial statements required by §§210.3-01 and 3-02. The schedule may be omitted if reserves for unpaid P/C claims and claims adjustment expenses of the registrant and its consolidated subsidiaries, its unconsolidated subsidiaries and its 50%-or-less-owned equity basis investees did not, in the aggregate, exceed one-half of common stockholders' equity of the registrant and its consolidated subsidiaries as of the beginning of the fiscal year. For purposes of this test only the proportionate share of the registrant and its other subsidiaries in the reserves for unpaid claims and claim adjustment expenses of 50%-or-less-owned equity basis investees taken in the aggregate after intercompany eliminations shall be taken into account.

[45 FR 63671, Sept. 25, 1980, as amended at 46 FR 48137, Oct. 1, 1981; 46 FR 56180, Nov. 16, 1981; 49 FR 47598, Dec. 6, 1984; 50 FR 25215, June 18, 1985; 59 FR 65636, Dec. 20, 1994; 74 FR 18615, Apr. 23, 2009]

Registered Investment Companies and Business Development Companies
Source: Sections 210.6-01 through 210.6-10 appear at 47 FR 56838, Dec. 21, 1982, unless otherwise noted.

§210.6-01 Application of §§210.6-01 to 210.6-10.
Sections 210.6-01 to 210.6-10 shall be applicable to financial statements filed for registered investment companies and business development companies.

[81 FR 82010, Nov. 18, 2016]

§210.6-02 Definition of certain terms.
Link to an amendment published at 81 FR 82137, Nov. 18, 2016.

The following terms shall have the meaning indicated in this rule unless the context otherwise requires. (Also see §210.1-02 of this part.)

(a) Affiliate. The term affiliate means an affiliated person as defined in section 2(a)(3) of the Investment Company Act of 1940 unless otherwise indicated. The term control has the meaning in section 2(a)(9) of that Act.

(b) Value. As used in §§210.6-01 to 210.6-10, the term value shall have the meaning given in section 2(a)(41)(B) of the Investment Company Act of 1940.

(c) Balance sheets; statements of net assets. As used in §§210.6-01 to 210.6-10, the term balance sheets shall include statements of assets and liabilities as well as statements of net assets unless the context clearly indicates the contrary.

(d) Qualified assets. (1) For companies issuing face-amount certificates subsequent to December 31, 1940 under the provisions of section 28 of the Investment Company Act of 1940, the term qualified assets means qualified investments as that term is defined in section 28(b) of the Act. A statement to that effect shall be made in the balance sheet.

(2) For other companies, the term qualified assets means cash and investments which such companies do maintain or are required, by applicable governing legal instruments, to maintain in respect of outstanding face-amount certificates.

(3) Loans to certificate holders may be included as qualified assets in an amount not in excess of certificate reserves carried on the books of account in respect of each individual certificate upon which the loans were made.

§210.6-03 Special rules of general application to registered investment companies and business development companies.
Link to an amendment published at 81 FR 82137, Nov. 18, 2016.

The financial statements filed for persons to which §§210.6-01 to 210.6-10 are applicable shall be prepared in accordance with the following special rules in addition to the general rules in §§210.1-01 to 210.4-10 (Articles 1, 2, 3, and 4). Where the requirements of a special rule differ from those prescribed in a general rule, the requirements of the special rule shall be met.

(a) Content of financial statements. The financial statements shall be prepared in accordance with the requirements of this part (Regulation S-X) notwithstanding any provision of the articles of incorporation, trust indenture or other governing legal instruments specifying certain accounting procedures inconsistent with those required in §§210.6-01 to 210.6-10.

(b) Audited financial statements. Where, under Article 3 of this part, financial statements are required to be audited, the independent accountant shall have been selected and ratified in accordance with section 32 of the Investment Company Act of 1940 (15 U.S.C. 80a-31).

(c) Consolidated and combined statements. (1) Consolidated and combined statements filed for registered investment companies and business development companies shall be prepared in accordance with §§210.3A-01 to 210.3A-04 (Article 3A) except that:

(i) Statements of the registrant may be consolidated only with the statements of subsidiaries which are investment companies;

(ii) A consolidated statement of the registrant and any of its investment company subsidiaries shall not be filed unless accompanied by a consolidating statement which sets forth the individual statements of each significant subsidiary included in the consolidated statement: Provided, however, That a consolidating statement need not be filed if all included subsidiaries are totally held; and

(iii) Consolidated or combined statements filed for subsidiaries not consolidated with the registrant shall not include any investment companies unless accompanied by consolidating or combining statements which set forth the individual statements of each included investment company which is a significant subsidiary.

(2) If consolidating or combining statements are filed, the amounts included under each caption in which financial data pertaining to affiliates is required to be furnished shall be subdivided to show separately the amounts:

(i) Eliminated in consolidation; and

(ii) Not eliminated in consolidation.

(d) Valuation of investments. The balance sheets of registered investment companies, other than issuers of face-amount certificates, and business development companies, shall reflect all investments at value, with the aggregate cost of each category of investment reported under §§210.6-04.1, 6-04.2, 6-04.3 and 6-04.9 or the aggregate cost of each category of investment reported under §210.6-05.1 shown parenthetically. State in a note the methods used in determining value of investments. As required by section 28(b) of the Investment Company Act of 1940 (15 U.S.C. 80a-28(b)), qualified assets of face-amount certificate companies shall be valued in accordance with certain provisions of the Code of the District of Columbia. For guidance as to valuation of securities, see §§404.03 to 404.05 of the Codification of Financial Reporting Policies.

(e) Qualified assets. State in a note the nature of any investments and other assets maintained or required to be maintained, by applicable legal instruments, in respect of outstanding face-amount certificates. If the nature of the qualifying assets and amount thereof are not subject to the provisions of section 28 of the Investment Company Act of 1940 (15 U.S.C. 80a-28), a statement to that effect shall be made.

(f) Restricted securities. State in a note unless disclosed elsewhere the following information as to investment securities which cannot be offered for public sale without first being registered under the Securities Act of 1933 (15 U.S.C. 77a et seq.) (restricted securities):

(1) The policy of the person with regard to acquisition of restricted securities.

(2) The policy of the person with regard to valuation of restricted securities. Specific comments shall be given as to the valuation of an investment in one or more issues of securities of a company or group of affiliated companies if any part of such investment is restricted and the aggregate value of the investment in all issues of such company or affiliated group exceeds five percent of the value of total assets. (As used in this paragraph, the term affiliated shall have the meaning given in §210.6-02(a).)

(3) A description of the person's rights with regard to demanding registration of any restricted securities held at the date of the latest balance sheet.

(g) Income recognition. Dividends shall be included in income on the ex-dividend date; interest shall be accrued on a daily basis. Dividends declared on short positions existing on the record date shall be recorded on the ex-dividend date and included as an expense of the period.

(h) Federal income taxes. (1) The company's status as a regulated investment company as defined in subtitle A, chapter 1, subchapter M of the Internal Revenue Code, as amended, shall be stated in a note referred to in the appropriate statements. Such note shall also indicate briefly the principal assumptions on which the company relied in making or not making provisions for income taxes. However, a company which retains realized capital gains and designates such gains as a distribution to shareholders in accordance with section 852(b)(3)(D) of the Internal Revenue Code shall, on the last day of its taxable year (and not earlier), make provision for taxes on such undistributed capital gains realized during such year.

(2) State the following amounts based on cost for Federal income tax purposes:

(i) Aggregate gross unrealized appreciation for all investments in which there is an excess of value over tax cost;

(ii) The aggregate gross unrealized depreciation for all investments in which there is an excess of tax cost over value;

(iii) The net unrealized appreciation or depreciation; and

(iv) The aggregate cost of investments for Federal income tax purposes.

(i) Issuance and repurchase by a registered investment company or business development company of its own securities. Disclose for each class of the company's securities:

(1) The number of shares, units, or principal amount of bonds sold during the period of report, the amount received therefor, and, in the case of shares sold by closed-end management investment companies, the difference, if any, between the amount received and the net asset value or preference in involuntary liquidation (whichever is appropriate) of securities of the same class prior to such sale; and

(2) The number of shares, units, or principal amount of bonds repurchased during the period of report and the cost thereof. Closed-end management investment companies shall furnish the following additional information as to securities repurchased during the period of report:

(i) As to bonds and preferred shares, the aggregate difference between cost and the face amount or preference in involuntary liquidation and, if applicable net assets taken at value as of the date of repurchase were less than such face amount or preference, the aggregate difference between cost and such net asset value;

(ii) As to common shares, the weighted average discount per share, expressed as a percentage, between cost of repurchase and the net asset value applicable to such shares at the date of repurchases.

Note to paragraphs (h)(2)(i) and (ii): The information required by paragraphs (h)(2)(i) and (ii) of this section may be based on reasonable estimates if it is impracticable to determine the exact amounts involved.

(j) Series companies. (1) The information required by this part shall, in the case of a person which in essence is comprised of more than one separate investment company, be given as if each class or series of such investment company were a separate investment company; this shall not prevent the inclusion, at the option of such person, of information applicable to other classes or series of such person on a comparative basis, except as to footnotes which need not be comparative.

(2) If the particular class or series for which information is provided may be affected by other classes or series of such investment company, such as by the offset of realized gains in one series with realized losses in another, or through contingent liabilities, such situation shall be disclosed.

(k) Certificate reserves. (1) For companies issuing face-amount certificates subsequent to December 31, 1940 under the provisions of section 28 of the Investment Company Act of 1940 (15 U.S.C. 80a-28), balance sheets shall reflect reserves for outstanding certificates computed in accordance with the provisions of section 28(a) of the Act.

(2) For other companies, balance sheets shall reflect reserves for outstanding certificates determined as follows:

(i) For certificates of the installment type, such amount which, together with the lesser of future payments by certificate holders as and when accumulated at a rate not to exceed 3 1/2 per centum per annum (or such other rate as may be appropriate under the circumstances of a particular case) compounded annually, shall provide the minimum maturity or face amount of the certificate when due.

(ii) For certificates of the fully-paid type, such amount which, as and when accumulated at a rate not to exceed 3 1⁄2 per centum per annum (or such other rate as may be appropriate under the circumstances of a particular case) compounded annually, shall provide the amount or amounts payable when due.

(iii) Such amount or accrual therefor, as shall have been credited to the account of any certificate holder in the form of any credit, or any dividend, or any interest in addition to the minimum maturity or face amount specified in the certificate, plus any accumulations on any amount so credited or accrued at rates required under the terms of the certificate.

(iv) An amount equal to all advance payments made by certificate holders, plus any accumulations thereon at rates required under the terms of the certificate.

(v) Amounts for other appropriate contingency reserves, for death and disability benefits or for reinstatement rights on any certificate providing for such benefits or rights.

(l) Inapplicable captions. Attention is directed to the provisions of §§210.4-02 and 210.4-03 which permit the omission of separate captions in financial statements as to which the items and conditions are not present, or the amounts involved not significant. However, amounts involving directors, officers, and affiliates shall nevertheless be separately set forth except as otherwise specifically permitted under a particular caption.

[81 FR 82010, Nov. 18, 2016]

§210.6-04 Balance sheets.

This section is applicable to balance sheets filed by registered investment companies and business development companies except for persons who substitute a statement of net assets in accordance with the requirements specified in §210.6-05, and issuers of face-amount certificates which are subject to the special provisions of §210.6-06. Balance sheets filed under this rule shall comply with the following provisions:

Assets

1. Investments in securities of unaffiliated issuers.

2. Investments in and advances to affiliates. State separately investments in and advances to: (a) Controlled companies and (b) other affiliates.

3. Other investments. State separately amounts of assets related to (a) variation margin receivable on futures contracts, (b) forward foreign currency contracts; (c) swap contracts; and (d) investments—other than those presented in §§210.12-12, 12-12A, 12-12B, 12-13, 12-13A, 12-13B, and 12-13C.

4. Cash. Include under this caption cash on hand and demand deposits. Provide in a note to the financial statements the information required under §210.5-02.1 regarding restrictions and compensating balances.

5. Receivables. (a) State separately amounts receivable from (1) sales of investments; (2) subscriptions to capital shares; (3) dividends and interest; (4) directors and officers; and (5) others.

(b) If the aggregate amount of notes receivable exceeds 10 percent of the aggregate amount of receivables, the above information shall be set forth separately, in the balance sheet or in a note thereto, for accounts receivable and notes receivable.

6. Deposits for securities sold short and other investments. State separately amounts held by others in connection with: (a) Short sales; (b) open option contracts (c) futures contracts, (d) forward foreign currency contracts; (e) swap contracts; and (f) investments—other than those presented in §§210.12-12, 12-12A, 12-12B, 12-13, 12-13A, 12-13B, and 12-13C.

7. Other assets. State separately (a) prepaid and deferred expenses; (b) pension and other special funds; (c) organization expenses; and (d) any other significant item not properly classified in another asset caption.

8. Total assets.

Liabilities
9. Other investments. State separately amounts of liabilities related to: (a) Securities sold short; (b) open option contracts written; (c) variation margin payable on futures contracts, (d) forward foreign currency contracts; (e) swap contracts; and (f) investments—other than those presented in §§210.12-12, 12-12A, 12-12B, 12-13, 12-13A, 12-13B, and 12-13C.

10. Accounts payable and accrued liabilities. State separately amounts payable for: (a) Other purchases of securities; (b) capital shares redeemed; (c) dividends or other distributions on capital shares; and (d) others. State separately the amount of any other liabilities which are material.

11. Deposits for securities loaned. State the value of securities loaned and indicate the nature of the collateral received as security for the loan, including the amount of any cash received.

12. Other liabilities. State separately (a) amounts payable for investment advisory, management and service fees; and (b) the total amount payable to: (1) Officers and directors; (2) controlled companies; and (3) other affiliates, excluding any amounts owing to noncontrolled affiliates which arose in the ordinary course of business and which are subject to usual trade terms.

13. Notes payable, bonds and similar debt. (a) State separately amounts payable to: (1) Banks or other financial institutions for borrowings; (2) controlled companies; (3) other affiliates; and (4) others, showing for each category amounts payable within one year and amounts payable after one year.

(b) Provide in a note the information required under §210.5-02.19(b) regarding unused lines of credit for short-term financing and §210.5-02.22(b) regarding unused commitments for long-term financing arrangements.

14. Total liabilities.

15. Commitments and contingent liabilities.

Net Assets
16. Units of capital. (a) Disclose the title of each class of capital shares or other capital units, the number authorized, the number outstanding, and the dollar amount thereof.

(b) Unit investment trusts, including those which are issuers of periodic payment plan certificates, also shall state in a note to the financial statements: (1) The total cost to the investors of each class of units or shares; (2) the adjustment for market depreciation or appreciation; (3) other deductions from the total cost to the investors for fees, loads and other charges, including an explanation of such deductions; and (4) the net amount applicable to the investors.

17. Accumulated undistributed income (loss). Disclose:

(a) The accumulated undistributed investment income-net,

(b) accumulated undistributed net realized gains (losses) on investment transactions, and (c) net unrealized appreciation (depreciation) in value of investments at the balance sheet date.

18. Other elements of capital. Disclose any other elements of capital or residual interests appropriate to the capital structure of the reporting entity.

19. Net assets applicable to outstanding units of capital. State the net asset value per share.

[81 FR 82011, Nov. 18, 2016]

§210.6-05 Statements of net assets.
In lieu of the balance sheet otherwise required by §210.6-04, persons may substitute a statement of net assets if at least 95 percent of the amount of the person's total assets are represented by investments in securities of unaffiliated issuers. If presented in such instances, a statement of net assets shall consist of the following:

Statements of Net Assets
1. A schedule of investments in securities of unaffiliated issuers as prescribed in §210.12-12.

2. The excess (or deficiency) of other assets over (under) total liabilities stated in one amount, except that any amounts due from or to officers, directors, controlled persons, or other affiliates,

excluding any amounts owing to noncontrolled affiliates which arose in the ordinary course of business and which are subject to usual trade terms, shall be stated separately.

3. Disclosure shall be provided in the notes to the financial statements for any item required under §210.6-04.3 and §§210.6-04.9 to 210.6-04.13.

4. The balance of the amounts captioned as net assets. The number of outstanding shares and net asset value per share shall be shown parenthetically.

5. The information required by (i) §210.6-04.16, (ii) §210.6-04.17 and (iii) §210.6-04.18 shall be furnished in a note to the financial statements.

[81 FR 82012, Nov. 18, 2016]

§210.6-06 Special provisions applicable to the balance sheets of issuers of face-amount certificates.

Balance sheets filed by issuers of face-amount certificates shall comply with the following provisions:

Assets

1. Investments. State separately each major category: such as, real estate owned, first mortgage loans on real estate, other mortgage loans on real estate, investments in securities of unaffiliated issuers, and investments in and advances to affiliates.

2. Cash. Include under this caption cash on hand and demand deposits. Provide in a note to the financial statements the information required under §210.5-02.1 regarding restrictions and compensating balances.

3. Receivables. (a) State separately amounts receivable from (1) sales of investments; (2) dividends and interest; (3) directors and officers; and (4) others.

(b) If the aggregate amount of notes receivable exceeds 10 percent of the aggregate amount of receivables, the above information shall be set forth separately, in the balance sheet or in a note thereto, for accounts receivable and notes receivable.

4. Total qualified assets. State in a note to the financial statements the amount of qualified assets on deposit classified as to general categories of assets and as to general types of depositories, such as banks and states, together with a statement as to the purpose of the deposits.

5. Other assets. State separately: (a) Investments in securities of unaffiliated issuers not included in qualifying assets in item 1 above; (b) investments in and advances to affiliates not included in qualifying assets in item 1 above; and (c) any other significant item not properly classified in another asset caption.

6. Total assets.

Liabilities

7. Certificate reserves. Issuers of face-amount certificates shall state separately reserves for: (a) Certificates of the installment type; (b) certificates of the fully-paid type; (c) advance payments; (d) additional amounts accrued for or credited to the account of certificate holders in the form of any credit, dividend, or interest in addition to the minimum amount specified in the certificate; and (e) other certificate reserves. State in an appropriate manner the basis used in determining the reserves, including the rates of interest of accumulation.

8. Notes payable, bonds and similar debt. (a) State separately amounts payable to: (1) Banks or other financial institutions for borrowings; (2) controlled companies; (3) other affiliates; and (4) others, showing for each category amounts payable within one year and amounts payable after one year.

(b) Provide in a note the information required under §210.5-02.19(b) regarding unused lines of credit for short-term financing and §210.5-02.22(b) regarding unused commitments for long-term financing arrangements.

9. Accounts payable and accrued liabilities. State separately (a) amounts payable for investment advisory, management and service fees; and (b) the total amount payable to: (1) Officers and directors; (2) controlled companies; and (3) other affiliates, excluding any amounts owing to noncontrolled affiliates which arose in the ordinary course of business and which are subject to usual trade terms. State separately the amount of any other liabilities which are material.

10. Total liabilities.

11. Commitments and contingent liabilities.

Stockholders' Equity

12. Capital shares. Disclose the title of each class of capital shares or other capital units, the number authorized, the number outstanding and the dollar amount thereof. Show also the dollar amount of any capital shares subscribed but unissued, and show the deduction for subscriptions receivable therefrom.

13. Other elements of capital. (a) Disclose any other elements of capital or residual interests appropriate to the capital structure of the reporting entity.

(b) A summary of each account under this caption setting forth the information prescribed in §210.3-04 shall be given in a note or separate statement for each period in which a statement of operations is presented.

14. Total liabilities and stockholders' equity.

§210.6-07 Statements of operations.

95

Statements of operations filed by registered investment companies, other than issuers of face-amount certificates, subject to the special provisions of §210.6-08, and business development companies, shall comply with the following provisions:

Statements of Operations
1. Investment income. State separately income from: (a) Dividends; (b) interest on securities; and (c) other income. Any other category of income which exceeds five percent of the total shown under this caption (e.g. income from non-cash dividends, income from payment-in-kind interest) shall be stated separately. If income from investments in or indebtedness of affiliates is included hereunder, such income shall be segregated under an appropriate caption subdivided to show separately income from: (1) Controlled companies; and (2) other affiliates. If income from non-cash dividends or payment in kind interest are included in income, the bases of recognition and measurement used in respect to such amounts shall be disclosed.

2. Expenses. (a) State separately the total amount of investment advisory, management and service fees, and expenses in connection with research, selection, supervision, and custody of investments. Amounts of expenses incurred from transactions with affiliated persons shall be disclosed together with the identity of and related amount applicable to each such person accounting for five percent or more of the total expenses shown under this caption together with a description of the nature of the affiliation. Expenses incurred within the person's own organization in connection with research, selection and supervision of investments shall be stated separately. Reductions or reimbursements of management or service fees shall be shown as a negative amount or as a reduction of total expenses shown under this caption.

(b) State separately any other expense item the amount of which exceeds five percent of the total expenses shown under this caption.

(c) A note to the financial statements shall include information concerning management and service fees, the rate of fee, and the base and method of computation. State separately the amount and a description of any fee reductions or reimbursements representing: (1) Expense limitation agreements or commitments; and (2) offsets received from broker-dealers showing separately for each amount received or due from (i) unaffiliated persons; and (ii) affiliated persons. If no management or service fees were incurred for a period, state the reason therefor.

(d) If any expenses were paid otherwise than in cash, state the details in a note.

(e) State in a note to the financial statements the amount of brokerage commissions (including dealer markups) paid to affiliated broker-dealers in connection with purchase and sale of investment securities. Open-end management companies shall state in a note the net amounts of sales charges deducted from the proceeds of sale of capital shares which were retained by any affiliated principal underwriter or other affiliated broker-dealer.

(f) State separately all amounts paid in accordance with a plan adopted under 17 CFR 270.12b-1 of this chapter. Reimbursement to the fund of expenses incurred under such plan (12b-1 expense reimbursement) shall be shown as a negative amount and deducted from current 12b-1 expenses.

If 12b-1 expense reimbursements exceed current 12b-1 costs, such excess shall be shown as a negative amount used in the calculation of total expenses under this caption.

(g)(1) Brokerage/Service Arrangements. If a broker-dealer or an affiliate of the broker-dealer has, in connection with directing the person's brokerage transactions to the broker-dealer, provided, agreed to provide, paid for, or agreed to pay for, in whole or in part, services provided to the person (other than brokerage and research services as those terms are used in section 28(e) of the Securities Exchange Act of 1934 [15 U.S.C. 78bb(e)]), include in the expense items set forth under this caption the amount that would have been incurred by the person for the services had it paid for the services directly in an arms-length transaction.

(2) Expense Offset Arrangements. If the person has entered into an agreement with any other person pursuant to which such other person reduces, or pays a third party which reduces, by a specified or reasonably ascertainable amount, its fees for services provided to the person in exchange for use of the person's assets, include in the expense items set forth under this caption the amount of fees that would have been incurred by the person if the person had not entered into the agreement.

(3) Financial Statement Presentation. Show the total amount by which expenses are increased pursuant to paragraphs (1) and (2) of this paragraph (2)(g) as a corresponding reduction in total expenses under this caption. In a note to the financial statements, state separately the total amounts by which expenses are increased pursuant to paragraphs (1) and (2) of this paragraph (2)(g), and list each category of expense that is increased by an amount equal to at least 5 percent of total expenses. If applicable, the note should state that the person could have employed the assets used by another person to produce income if it had not entered into an arrangement described in paragraph (2)(g)(2) of this section.

3. Interest and amortization of debt discount and expense. Provide in the body of the statements or in the footnotes, the average dollar amount of borrowings and the average interest rate.

4. Investment income before income tax expense.

5. Income tax expense. Include under this caption only taxes based on income.

6. Investment income-net.

7. Realized and unrealized gain (loss) on investments-net. (a) State separately the net realized gain or loss from: (1) Transactions in investment securities of unaffiliated issuers, (2) transactions in investment securities of affiliated issuers, (3) expiration or closing of option contracts written, (4) closed short positions in securities, (5) expiration or closing of futures contracts, (6) settlement of forward foreign currency contracts, (7) expiration or closing of swap contracts, and (8) transactions in other investments held during the period.

(b) Distributions of realized gains by other investment companies shall be shown separately under this caption.

(c) State separately the amount of the net increase or decrease during the period in the unrealized appreciation or depreciation in the value of: (1) Investment securities of unaffiliated issuers, (2) investment securities of affiliated issuers, (3) option contracts written, (4) short positions in securities, (5) futures contracts, (6) forward foreign currency contracts, (7) swap contracts, and (8) other investments held at the end of the period.

(d) State separately any: (1) Federal income taxes and (2) other income taxes applicable to realized and unrealized gain (loss) on investments, distinguishing taxes payable currently from deferred income taxes.

8. Net gain (loss) on investments.

9. Net increase (decrease) in net assets resulting from operations.

[81 FR 82012, Nov. 18, 2016]

§210.6-08 Special provisions applicable to the statements of operations of issuers of face-amount certificates.

Statements of operations filed by issuers of face-amount certificates shall comply with the following provisions:

Statements of Operations

1. Investment income. State separately income from: (a) Interest on mortgages; (b) interest on securities; (c) dividends; (d) rental income; and (e) other investment income. If income from investments in or indebtedness of affiliates is included hereunder, such income shall be segregated under an appropriate caption subdivided to show separately income from: (1) Controlled companies; and (2) other affiliates. If non-cash dividends are included in income, the bases of recognition and measurement used in respect to such amounts shall be disclosed. Any other category of income which exceeds five percent of the total shown under this caption shall be stated separately.

2. Investment expenses. (a) State separately the total amount of investment advisory, management and service fees, and expenses in connection with research, selection, supervision, and custody of investments. Amounts of expenses incurred from transactions with affiliated persons shall be disclosed together with the identity of and related amount applicable to each such person accounting for five percent or more of the total expenses shown under this caption together with a description of the nature of the affiliation. Expenses incurred within the person's own organization in connection with research, selection and supervision of investments shall be stated separately. Reductions or reimbursements of management or service fees shall be shown as a negative amount or as a reduction of total expenses shown under this caption.

(b) State separately any other expense item the amount of which exceeds five percent of the total expenses shown under this caption.

(c) A note to the financial statements shall include information concerning management and service fees, the rate of fee, and the base and method of computation. State separately the amount and a description of any fee reductions or reimbursements representing: (1) Expense limitation agreements or commitments; and (2) offsets received from broker-dealers showing separately for each amount received or due from: (i) Unaffiliated persons; and (ii) affiliated persons. If no management or service fees were incurred for a period, state the reason therefor.

(d) If any expenses were paid otherwise than in cash, state the details in a note.

(e) State in a note to the financial statements the amount of brokerage commissions (including dealer markups) paid to affiliated broker-dealers in connection with purchase and sale of investment securities.

3. Interest and amortization of debt discount and expense.

4. Provision for certificate reserves. State separately any provision for additional credits, or dividends, or interests, in addition to the minimum maturity or face amount specified in the certificates. State also in an appropriate manner reserve recoveries from surrenders or other causes.

5. Investment income before income tax expense.

6. Income tax expense. Include under this caption only taxes based on income.

7. Investment income-net.

8. Realized gain (loss) on investments-net.

(a) State separately the net realized gain or loss on transactions in: (1) Investment securities of unaffiliated issuers, (2) investment securities of affiliated issuers, and (3) other investments.

(b) Distributions of capital gains by other investment companies shall be shown separately under this caption.

(c) State separately any: (1) Federal income taxes and (2) other income taxes applicable to realized gain (loss) on investments, distinguishing taxes payable currently from deferred income taxes.

9. Net income or loss.

§210.6-09 Statements of changes in net assets.
Statements of changes in net assets filed for persons to whom this article is applicable shall comply with the following provisions:

Statements of Changes in Net Assets

1. Operations. State separately: (a) Investment income-net as shown by §210.6-07.6; (b) realized gain (loss) on investments-net of any Federal or other income taxes applicable to such amounts; (c) increase (decrease) in unrealized appreciation or depreciation-net of any Federal or other income taxes applicable to such amounts; and (d) net increase (decrease) in net assets resulting from operations as shown by §210.6-07.9.

2. Net equalization charges and credits. State the net amount of accrued undivided earnings separately identified in the price of capital shares issued and repurchased.

3. Distributions to shareholders. State separately distributions to shareholders from: (a) Investment income-net; (b) realized gain from investment transactions-net; and (c) other sources.

4. Capital share transactions. (a) State the increase or decrease in net assets derived from the net change in the number of outstanding shares or units.

(b) Disclose in the body of the statements or in the notes, for each class of the person's shares, the number and value of shares issued in reinvestment of dividends as well as the number of dollar amounts received for shares sold and paid for shares redeemed.

5. Total increase (decrease).

6. Net assets at the beginning of the period.

7. Net assets at the end of the period. Disclose parenthetically the balance of undistributed net investment income included in net assets at the end of the period.

§210.6-10 What schedules are to be filed.
(a) When information is required in schedules for both the person and its subsidiaries consolidated, it may be presented in the form of a single schedule, provided that items pertaining to the registrant are separately shown and that such single schedule affords a properly summarized presentation of the facts.

(b) The schedules shall be examined by an independent accountant if the related financial statements are so examined.

(c) Management investment companies. (1) Except as otherwise provided in the applicable form, the schedules specified in this paragraph shall be filed for management investment companies as of the dates of the most recent audited balance sheet and any subsequent unaudited statement being filed for each person or group.

Schedule I—Investments in securities of unaffiliated issuers. The schedule prescribed by §210.12-12 shall be filed in support of caption 1 of each balance sheet.

Schedule II—Investments in and advances to affiliates. The schedule prescribed by §210.12-14 shall be filed in support of caption 2 of each balance sheet.

Schedule III—Investments—securities sold short. The schedule prescribed by §210.12-12A shall be filed in support of caption 9(a) of each balance sheet.

Schedule IV—Open option contracts written. The schedule prescribed by §210.12-13 shall be filed in support of caption 9(b) of each balance sheet.

Schedule V—Open futures contracts. The schedule prescribed by §210.12-13A shall be filed in support of captions 3(a) and 9(c) of each balance sheet.

Schedule VI—Open forward foreign currency contracts. The schedule prescribed by §210.12-13B shall be filed in support of captions 3(b) and 9(d) of each balance sheet.

Schedule VII—Open swap contracts. The schedule prescribed by §210.12-13C shall be filed in support of captions 3(c) and 9(e) of each balance sheet.

Schedule VIII—Investments—other than those presented in §§210.12-12, 12-12A, 12-12B, 12-13, 12-13A, 12-13B and 12-13C. The schedule prescribed by §210.12-13D shall be filed in support of captions 3(d) and 9(f) of each balance sheet.

(2) When permitted by the applicable form, the schedule specified in this paragraph may be filed for management investment companies as of the dates of the most recent audited balance sheet and any subsequent unaudited statement being filed for each person or group.

Schedule IX—Summary schedule of investments in securities of unaffiliated issuers. The schedule prescribed by §210.12-12B may be filed in support of caption 1 of each balance sheet.

(d) Unit investment trusts. Except as otherwise provided in the applicable form:

(1) Schedules I and II, specified below in this section, shall be filed for unit investment trusts as of the dates of the most recent audited balance sheet and any subsequent unaudited statement being filed for each person or group.

(2) Schedule III, specified below in this section, shall be filed for unit investment trusts for each period for which a statement of operations is required to be filed for each person or group.

Schedule I—Investment in securities. The schedule prescribed by §210.12-12 shall be filed in support of caption 1 of each balance sheet (§210.6-04).

Schedule II—Allocation of trust assets to series of trust shares. If the trust assets are specifically allocated to different series of trust shares, and if such allocation is not shown in the balance sheet in columnar form or by the filing of separate statements for each series of trust shares, a schedule shall be filed showing the amount of trust assets, indicated by each balance sheet filed, which is applicable to each series of trust shares.

Schedule III—Allocation of trust income and distributable funds to series of trust shares. If the trust income and distributable funds are specifically allocated to different series of trust shares and if such allocation is not shown in the statement of operations in columnar form or by the filing of separate statements for each series of trust shares, a schedule shall be submitted showing the amount of income and distributable funds, indicated by each statement of operations filed, which is applicable to each series of trust shares.

(e) Face-amount certificate investment companies. Except as otherwise provided in the applicable form:

(1) Schedules I, V and X, specified below, shall be filed for face-amount certificate investment companies as of the dates of the most recent audited balance sheet and any subsequent unaudited statement being filed for each person or group.

(2) All other schedules specified below in this section shall be filed for face-amount certificate investment companies for each period for which a statement of operations is filed, except as indicated for Schedules III and IV.

Schedule I—Investment in securities of unaffiliated issuers. The schedule prescribed by §210.12-21 shall be filed in support of caption 1 and, if applicable, caption 5(a) of each balance sheet. Separate schedules shall be furnished in support of each caption, if applicable.

Schedule II—Investments in and advances to affiliates and income thereon. The schedule prescribed by §210.12-22 shall be filed in support of captions 1 and 5(b) of each balance sheet and caption 1 of each statement of operations. Separate schedules shall be furnished in support of each caption, if applicable.

Schedule III—Mortgage loans on real estate and interest earned on mortgages. The schedule prescribed by §210.12-23 shall be filed in support of captions 1 and 5(c) of each balance sheet and caption 1 of each statement of operations, except that only the information required by Column G and note 8 of the schedule need be furnished in support of statements of operations for years for which related balance sheets are not required.

Schedule IV—Real estate owned and rental income. The schedule prescribed by §210.12-24 shall be filed in support of captions 1 and 5(a) of each balance sheet and caption 1 of each statement of operations for rental income included therein, except that only the information required by Columns H, I and J, and item "Rent from properties sold during the period" and note 4 of the schedule need be furnished in support of statements of operations for years for which related balance sheets are not required.

Schedule V—Qualified assets on deposit. The schedule prescribed by §210.12-27 shall be filed in support of the information required by caption 4 of §210.6-06 as to total amount of qualified assets on deposit.

Schedule VI—Certificate reserves. The schedule prescribed by §210.12-26 shall be filed in support of caption 7 of each balance sheet.

Schedule VII—Valuation and qualifying accounts. The schedule prescribed by §210.12-09 shall be filed in support of all other reserves included in the balance sheet.

[81 FR 82013, Nov. 18, 2016]

Employee Stock Purchase, Savings and Similar Plans

§210.6A-01   Application of §§210.6A-01 to 210.6A-05.
(a) Sections 210.6A-01 to 210.6A-05 shall be applicable to financial statements filed for employee stock purchase, savings and similar plans.

(b) [Reserved]

[47 FR 56843, Dec. 21, 1982]

§210.6A-02   Special rules applicable to employee stock purchase, savings and similar plans.
The financial statements filed for persons to which this article is applicable shall be prepared in accordance with the following special rules in addition to the general rules in §§210.1-01 to 210.4-10. Where the requirements of a special rule differ from those prescribed in a general rule, the requirements of the special rule shall be met.

(a) Investment programs. If the participating employees have an option as to the manner in which their deposits and contributions may be invested, a description of each investment program shall be given in a footnote or otherwise. The number of employees under each investment program shall be stated.

(b) Net asset value per unit. Where appropriate, the number of units and the net asset value per unit shall be given by footnote or otherwise.

(c) Federal income taxes. (1) If the plan is not subject to Federal income taxes, a note shall so state indicating briefly the principal assumptions on which the plan relied in not making provision for such taxes.

(2) State the Federal income tax status of the employee with respect to the plan.

(d) Valuation of assets. The statement of financial condition shall reflect all investments at value, showing cost parenthetically. For purposes of this rule, the term value shall mean (1) market value for those securities having readily available market quotations and (2) fair value as determined in good faith by the trustee(s) for the plan (or by the person or persons who exercise similar responsibilities) with respect to other securities and assets.

103

[47 FR 56843, Dec. 21, 1982]

§210.6A-03 Statements of financial condition.

Statements of financial condition filed under this rule shall comply with the following provisions:

Plan Assets

1. Investments in securities of participating employers. State separately each class of securities of the participating employer or employers.

2. Investments in securities of unaffiliated issuers.

(a) United States Government bonds and other obligations. Include only direct obligations of the United States Government.

(b) Other securities. State separately (1) marketable securities and (2) other securities.

3. Investments. Other than securities. State separately each major class.

4. Dividends and interest receivable.

5. Cash.

6. Other assets. State separately (a) total of amounts due from participating employers or any of their directors, officers and principal holders of equity securities; (b) total of amounts due from trustees or managers of the plan; and (c) any other significant amounts.

Liabilities and Plan Equity

7. Liabilities. State separately (a) total of amounts payable to participating employers; (b) total of amounts payable to participating employees; and (c) any other significant amounts.

8. Reserves and other credits. State separately each significant item and describe each such item by using an appropriate caption or by a footnote referred to in the caption.

9. Plan equity at close of period.

[27 FR 7870, Aug. 9, 1962. Redesignated at 47 FR 56843, Dec. 21, 1982]

§210.6A-04 Statements of income and changes in plan equity.

Statements of income and changes in plan equity filed under this rule shall comply with the following provisions:

1. Net investment income.

(a) Income. State separately income from (1) cash dividends; (2) interest, and (3) other sources. Income from investments in or indebtedness of participating employers shall be segregated under the appropriate subcaption.

(b) Expenses. State separately any significant amounts.

(c) Net investment income.

2. Realized gain or loss on investments. (a) State separately the net of gains or losses arising from transactions in (1) investments in securities of the participating employer or employers; (2) other investments in securities; and (3) other investments.

(b) State in a footnote or otherwise for each category of investment in paragraph (a) above the aggregate cost, the aggregate proceeds and the net gain or loss. State the principle followed in determining the cost of securities sold, e.g., average cost or first-in, first-out.

3. Unrealized appreciation or depreciation of investments. (a) State the amount of increase or decrease in unrealized appreciation or depreciation of investments during the period.

(b) State in a footnote or otherwise the amount of unrealized appreciation or depreciation of investments at the beginning of the period of report, at the end of the period of report, and the increase or decrease during the period.

4. Contributions and deposits. (a) State separately (1) total of amounts deposited by participating employees, and (2) total of amounts contributed by the participating employer or employers.

(b) If employees of more than one employer participate in the plan, state in tabular form in a footnote or otherwise the amount contributed by each employer and the deposits of the employees of each such employer.

5. Withdrawals, lapses and forfeitures. State separately (a) balances of employees' accounts withdrawn, lapsed or forfeited during the period; (b) amounts disbursed in settlement of such accounts; and (c) disposition of balances remaining after settlement specified in (b).

6. Plan equity at beginning of period.

7. Plan equity at end of period.

[27 FR 7870, Aug. 9, 1962. Redesignated at 47 FR 56843, Dec. 21, 1982]

§210.6A-05 What schedules are to be filed.
(a) Schedule I, specified below, shall be filed as of the most recent audited statement of financial condition and any subsequent unaudited statement of financial condition being filed. Schedule II shall be filed as of the date of each statement of financial condition being filed. Schedule III shall

be filed for each period for which a statement of income and changes in plan equity is filed. All schedules shall be audited if the related statements are audited.

Schedule I—Investments. A schedule substantially in form prescribed by §210.12-12 shall be filed in support of captions 1, 2 and 3 of each statement of financial condition unless substantially all of the information is given in the statement of financial condition by footnote or otherwise.

Schedule II—Allocation of plan assets and liabilities to investment program. If the plan provides for separate investment programs with separate funds, and if the allocation of assets and liabilities to the several funds is not shown in the statement of financial condition in columnar form or by the submission of separate statements for each fund, a schedule shall be submitted showing the allocation of each caption of each statement of financial condition filed to the applicable fund.

Schedule III—Allocation of plan income and changes in plan equity to investment programs. If the plan provides for separate investment programs with separate funds, and if the allocation of income and changes in plan equity to the several funds is not shown in the statement of income and changes in plan equity in columnar form or by the submission of separate statements for each fund, a schedule shall be submitted showing the allocation of each caption of each statement of income and changes in plan equity filed to the applicable fund.

(b) [Reserved]

[45 FR 63676, Sept. 25, 1980. Redesignated at 47 FR 56843, Dec. 21, 1982, and amended at 50 FR 25215, June 18, 1985]

Insurance Companies
Source: Sections 210.7-01 through 210.7-05 appears at 46 FR 54335, Nov. 2, 1981, unless otherwise noted.

§210.7-01   Application of §§210.7-01 to 210.7-05.
This article shall be applicable to financial statements filed for insurance companies.

§210.7-02   General requirement.
(a) The requirements of the general rules in §§210.1-01 to 210.4-10 (Articles 1, 2, 3, 3A and 4) shall be applicable except where they differ from requirements of §§210.7-01 to 210.7-05.

(b) Financial statements filed for mutual life insurance companies and wholly owned stock insurance company subsidiaries of mutual life insurance companies may be prepared in accordance with statutory accounting requirements. Financial statements prepared in accordance with statutory accounting requirements may be condensed as appropriate, but the amounts to be reported for net gain from operations (or net income or loss) and total capital and surplus (or surplus as regards policyholders) shall be the same as those reported on the corresponding Annual Statement.

§210.7-03 Balance sheets.

(a) The purpose of this rule is to indicate the various items which, if applicable, and except as otherwise permitted by the Commission, should appear on the face of the balance sheets and in the notes thereto filed for persons to whom this article pertains. (See §210.4-01(a).)

Assets

1. Investments—other than investments in related parties.

(a) Fixed maturities.

(b) Equity securities.

(c) Mortgage loans on real estate.

(d) Investment real estate.

(e) Policy loans.

(f) Other long-term investments.

(g) Short-term investments.

(h) Total investments.

Notes: (1) State parenthetically or otherwise in the balance sheet (a) the basis of determining the amounts shown in the balance sheet and (b) as to fixed maturities and equity securities either aggregate cost or aggregate value at the balance sheet date, whichever is the alternate amount of the carrying value in the balance sheet. Consideration shall be given to the discussion of "Valuation of Securities" in §404.03 of the Codification of Financial Reporting Policies.

(2) Include under fixed maturities: bonds, notes, marketable certificates of deposit with maturities beyond one year, and redeemable preferred stocks. Include under equity securities: common stocks and nonredeemable preferred stocks.

(3) State separately in the balance sheet or in a note thereto the amount of accumulated depreciation and amortization deducted from investment real estate. Subcaption (d) shall not include real estate acquired in settling title claims, mortgage guaranty claims, and similar insurance claims. Real estate acquired in settling claims shall be included in caption 10, "Other Assets," or shown separately, if material.

(4) Include under subcaption (g) investments maturing within one year, such as commercial paper maturing within one year, marketable certificates of deposit maturing within one year,

savings accounts, time deposits and other cash accounts and cash equivalents earning interest. State in a note any amounts subject to withdrawal or usage restrictions. (See §210.5-02.1.)

(5) State separately in a note the amount of any class of investments included in subcaption (f) if such amount exceeds ten percent of stockholders' equity.

(6) State in a note the name of any person in which the total amount invested in the person and its affiliates, included in the above subcaptions, exceeds ten percent of total stockholders' equity. For this disclosure, include in the amount invested in a person and its affiliates the aggregate of indebtedness and stocks issued by such person and its affiliates that is included in the several subcaptions above, and the amount of any real estate included in subcaption (d) that was purchased or acquired from such person and its affiliates. Indicate the amount included in each subcaption. An investment in bonds and notes of the United States Government or of a United States Government agency or authority which exceeds ten percent of total stockholders' equity need not be reported.

(7) State in a note the amount of investments included under each subcaption (a), (c), (d) and (f) which have been non-income producing for the twelve months preceding the balance sheet date.

2. Cash. Cash on hand or on deposit that is restricted as to withdrawal or usage shall be disclosed separately on the balance sheet. The provisions of any restrictions shall be described in a note to the financial statements. Restrictions may include legally restricted deposits held as compensating balances against short-term borrowing arrangements, contracts entered into with others, or company statements of intention with regard to particular deposits. In cases where compensating balance arrangements exist but are not agreements which legally restrict the use of cash amounts shown on the balance sheet, describe in the notes to the financial statements these arrangements and the amount involved, if determinable, for the most recent audited balance sheet required. Compensating balances that are maintained under an agreement to assure future credit availability shall be disclosed in the notes to the financial statements along with the amount and terms of the agreement.

3. Securities and indebtedness of related parties. State separately (a) investments in related parties and (b) indebtedness from such related parties. (See §210.4-08(k).)

4. Accrued investment income.

5. Accounts and notes receivable. Include under this caption (a) amounts receivable from agents and insureds, (b) uncollected premiums and (c) other receivables. State separately in the balance sheet or in a note thereto any category of other receivable which is in excess of five percent of total assets. State separately in the balance sheet or in a note thereto the amount of allowance for doubtful accounts that was deducted.

6. Reinsurance recoverable on paid losses.

7. Deferred policy acquisition costs.

8. Property and equipment. (a) State the basis of determining the amounts.

(b) State separately in the balance sheet or in a note thereto the amount of accumulated depreciation and amortization of property and equipment.

9. Title plant.

10. Other assets. State separately in the balance sheet or in a note thereto any other asset the amount of which exceeds five percent of total assets.

11. Assets held in separate accounts. Include under this caption the aggregate amount of assets used to fund liabilities related to variable annuities, pension funds and similar activities. The aggregate liability shall be included under caption 18. Describe in a note to the financial statements the general nature of the activities being reported on in the separate accounts.

12. Total assets.

Liabilities and Stockholders' Equity

13. Policy liabilities and accruals. (a) State separately in the balance sheet the amounts of (1) future policy benefits and losses, claims and loss expenses, (2) unearned premiums and (3) other policy claims and benefits payable.

(b) State in a note to the financial statements the basis of assumptions (interest rates, mortality, withdrawals) for future policy benefits and claims and settlements which are stated at present value.

(c) Information shall be given in a note concerning the general nature of reinsurance transactions, including a description of the significant types of reinsurance agreements executed. The information provided shall include (1) the nature of the contingent liability in connection with insurance ceded and (2) the nature and effect of material nonrecurring reinsurance transactions.

14. Other policyholders' funds. (a) Include amounts of supplementary contracts without life contingencies, policyholders' dividend accumulations, undistributed earnings on participating business, dividends to policyholders and retrospective return premiums (not included elsewhere) and any similar items. State separately in the balance sheet or in a note thereto any item the amount of which is in excess of five percent of total liabilities.

(b) State in a note to the financial statements the relative significance of participating insurance expressed as percentages of (1) insurance in force and (2) premium income; and the method by which earnings and dividends allocable to such insurance is determined.

15. Other liabilities. (a) Include under this caption such items as accrued payrolls, accrued interest and taxes. State separately in the balance sheet or in a note thereto any item included in other liabilities the amount of which exceeds five percent of total liabilities.

(b) State separately in the balance sheet or in a note thereto the amount of (1) income taxes payable and (2) deferred income taxes. Disclose separately the amount of deferred income taxes applicable to unrealized appreciation of equity securities.

16. Notes payable, bonds, mortgages and similar obligations, including capitalized leases. (a) State separately in the balance sheet the amounts of (1) short-term debt and (2) long-term debt including capitalized leases.

(b) The disclosure required by §210.5-02.19(b) shall be given if the aggregate of short-term borrowings from banks, factors and other financial institutions and commercial paper issued exceeds five percent of total liabilities.

(c) The disclosure requirements of §210.5-02.22 shall be followed for long-term debt.

17. Indebtedness to related parties. (See §210.4-0.8(k).)

18. Liabilities related to separate accounts. [See caption 11.]

19. Commitments and contingent liabilities.

Redeemable Preferred Stocks
20. Preferred stocks subject to mandatory redemption requirements or whose redemption is outside the control of the issuer. The classification and disclosure requirements of §210.5-02.27 shall be followed.

Nonredeemable Preferred Stocks
21. Preferred stocks which are not redeemable or are redeemable solely at the option of the issuer. The classification and disclosure requirements of §210.5-02.28 shall be followed.

Common Stocks
22. Common stocks. The classification and disclosure requirements of §210.5-02.29 shall be followed.

Other Stockholders' Equity
23. Other stockholders' equity. (a) Separate captions shall be shown for (1) additional paid-in capital, (2) other additional capital, (3) unrealized appreciation or depreciation of equity securities less applicable deferred income taxes, (4) retained earnings (i) appropriated and (ii) unappropriated. (See §210.4-08(e).) Additional paid-in capital and other additional capital may be combined with the stock caption to which they apply, if appropriate.

(b) The classification and disclosure requirements of §210.5-02.30(b) shall be followed for dating and effect of a quasi-reorganization.

(c) State in a note the following information separately for (1) life insurance legal entities, and (2) property and liability insurance legal entities: the amount of statutory stockholders' equity as of the date of each balance sheet presented and the amount of statutory net income or loss for each period for which an income statement is presented.

Noncontrolling Interests
24. Noncontrolling interests in consolidated subsidiaries. The disclosure requirements of §210.5-02.31 shall be followed.

25. Total liabilities and equity.

[46 FR 54335, Nov. 2, 1981, as amended at 50 FR 25215, June 18, 1985; 74 FR 18615, Apr. 23, 2009]

§210.7-04   Income statements.

The purpose of this rule is to indicate the various items which, if applicable, should appear on the face of the income statements and in the notes thereto filed for persons to whom this article pertains. (See §210.4-01(a).)

Revenues

1. Premiums. Include premiums from reinsurance assumed and deduct premiums on reinsurance ceded. Where applicable, the amounts included in this caption should represent premiums earned.

2. Net investment income. State in a note to the financial statements, in tabular form, the amounts of (a) investment income from each category of investments listed in the subcaptions of §210.7-03.1 that exceeds five percent of total investment income, (b) total investment income, (c) applicable expenses, and (d) net investment income.

3. Realized investment gains and losses. Disclose the following amounts:

(a) Net realized investment gains and losses, which shall be shown separately regardless of size.

(b) Indicate in a footnote the registrant's policy with respect to whether investment income and realized gains and losses allocable to policyholders and separate accounts are included in the investment income and realized gain and loss amounts reported in the income statement. If the income statement includes investment income and realized gains and losses allocable to policyholders and separate accounts, indicate the amounts of such allocable investment income and realized gains and losses and the manner in which the insurance enterprise's obligation with respect to allocation of such investment income and realized gains and losses is otherwise accounted for in the financial statements.

(c) The method followed in determining the cost of investments sold (e.g., "average cost," "first-in, first-out," or "identified certificate") shall be disclosed.

(d) For each period for which an income statement is filed, include in a note an analysis of realized and unrealized investment gains and losses on fixed maturities and equity securities. For each period, state separately for fixed maturities [see §210.7-03.1(a)] and for equity securities [see §210.7-03.1(b)] the following amounts:

(1) Realized investment gains and losses, and

(2) The change during the period in the difference between value and cost.

The change in the difference between value and cost shall be given for both categories of investments even though they may be shown on the related balance sheet on a basis other than value.

4. Other income. Include all revenues not included in captions 1 and 2 above. State separately in the statement any amounts in excess of five percent of total revenue, and disclose the nature of the transactions from which the items arose.

Benefits, Losses and Expenses

5. Benefits, claims, losses and settlement expenses.

6. Policyholders' share of earnings on participating policies, dividends and similar items. (See §210.7-03.14(b).)

7. Underwriting, acquisition and insurance expenses. State separately in the income statement or in a note thereto (a) the amount included in this caption representing deferred policy acquisition costs amortized to income during the period, and (b) the amount of other operating expenses. State separately in the income statement any material amount included in all other operating expenses.

8. Income or loss before income tax expense and appropriate items below.

9. Income tax expense. Include under this caption only taxes based on income. (See §210.4-08(g).)

10. Equity in earnings of unconsolidated subsidiaries and 50% or less owned persons. State, parenthetically or in a note, the amount of dividends received from such persons. If justified by the circumstances, this item may be presented in a different position and a different manner. (See §210.4-01(a).)

11. Income or loss from continuing operations.

12. Discontinued operations.

13. Income or loss before extraordinary items and cumulative effects of changes in accounting principles.

14. Extraordinary items, less applicable tax.

15. Cumulative effects of changes in accounting principles.

16. Net income or loss.

17. Net income attributable to the noncontrolling interest.

18. Net income attributable to the controlling interest.

19. Earnings per share data.

[46 FR 54335, Nov. 2, 1981, as amended at 57 FR 45293, Oct. 1, 1992; 74 FR 18615, Apr. 23, 2009]

§210.7-05 What schedules are to be filed.

(a) Except as expressly provided otherwise in the applicable form:

(1) The schedule specified below in this section as Schedules I shall be as of the date of the most recent audited balance sheet for each person or group.

(2) The schedules specified below in this section as Schedule IV and V shall be filed for each period for which an audited income statement is required to be filed for each person or group.

(3) Schedules II, III and V shall be filed as of the date and for periods specified in the schedule.

(b) When information is required in schedules for both the registrant and the registrant and its subsidiaries consolidated it may be presented in the form of a single schedule: Provided, That items pertaining to the registrant are shown separately and that such single schedule affords a properly summarized presentation of the facts. If the information required by any schedule (including the notes thereto) may be shown in the related financial statement or in a note thereto without making such statement unclear or confusing, that procedure may be followed and the schedule omitted.

(c) The schedules shall be examined by the independent accountant.

Schedule I—Summary of investments—other than investments in related parties. The schedule prescribed by §210.12-15 shall be filed in support of caption 1 of the most recent audited balance sheet.

Schedule II—Condensed financial information of registrant. The schedule prescribed by §210.12-04 shall be filed when the restricted net assets (§210.4.08(e)(3)) of consolidated subsidiaries exceed 25 percent of consolidated net assets as of the end of the most recently completed fiscal year. For purposes of the above test, restricted net assets of consolidated subsidiaries shall mean that amount of the registrant's proportionate share of net assets of consolidated subsidiaries (after intercompany eliminations) which as of the end of the most recent fiscal year may not be transferred to the parent company by subsidiaries in the form of loans, advances or cash dividends without the consent of a third party (i.e., lender, regulatory agency, foreign government, etc.). Where restrictions on the amount of funds which may be loaned or advanced differ from the amount restricted as to transfer in the form of cash dividends, the amount least restrictive to the subsidiary shall be used. Redeemable preferred stocks (§210.7-03.20) and noncontrolling interests shall be deducted in computing net assets for purposes of this test.

Schedule III—Supplementary insurance information. The schedule prescribed by §210.12-16 shall be filed giving segment detail in support of various balance sheet and income statement captions. The required balance sheet information shall be presented as of the date of each audited balance sheet filed, and the income statement information shall be presented for each period for which an audited income statement is required to be filed, for each person or group.

Schedule IV—Reinsurance. The schedule prescribed by §210.12-17 shall be filed for reinsurance ceded and assumed.

Schedule V—Valuation and qualifying accounts. The schedule prescribed by §210.12-09 shall be filed in support of valuation and qualifying accounts included in the balance sheet (see §210.4-02).

Schedule VI—Supplemental Information Concerning Property-Casualty Insurance Operations. The information required by §210.12-18 shall be presented as of the same dates and for the same periods for which the information is reflected in the audited consolidated financial statements required by §§210.3-01 and 3-02. The schedule may be omitted if reserves for unpaid property-casualty claims and claim adjustment expenses of the registrant and its consolidated subsidiaries, its unconsolidated subsidiaries and its 50%-or-less-owned equity basis investees did not in the aggregate, exceed one-half of common stockholders' equity of the registrant and its consolidated subsidiaries as of the beginning of the fiscal year. For purposes of this test, only the proportionate share of the registrant and its other subsidiaries in the reserves for unpaid claims and claim adjustment expenses of 50%-or-less-owned equity investees taken in the aggregate after intercompany eliminations shall be taken into account. Article 12—Form and Content of Schedules (17 CFR 210)

[46 FR 54335, Nov. 2, 1981, as amended at 47 FR 29837, July 9, 1982; 49 FR 47598, Dec. 6, 1984; 59 FR 65637, Dec. 20, 1994; 74 FR 18615, Apr. 23, 2009]

Article 8 Financial Statements of Smaller Reporting Companies
Source: 73 FR 953, Jan. 4, 2008, unless otherwise noted.

§210.8-01 Preliminary Notes to Article 8.
Sections 210.8-01 to 210.8-08 shall be applicable to financial statements filed for smaller reporting companies. These sections are not applicable to financial statements prepared for the purposes of Item 17 or Item 18 of Form 20-F.

Note 1 to §210.8: Financial statements of a smaller reporting company, as defined by §229.10(f)(1) of this chapter, its predecessors or any businesses to which the smaller reporting company is a successor shall be prepared in accordance with generally accepted accounting principles in the United States.

Note 2 to §210.8: Smaller reporting companies electing to prepare their financial statements with the form and content required in this article need not apply the other form and content requirements in Regulation S-X with the exception of the following:

a. The report and qualifications of the independent accountant shall comply with the requirements of Article 2 of this part;

b. The description of accounting policies shall comply with Article 4-08(n) of this part; and

c. Smaller reporting companies engaged in oil and gas producing activities shall follow the financial accounting and reporting standards specified in Article 4-10 of this part with respect to such activities.

To the extent that Article 11-01 of this part (Pro Forma Presentation Requirements) offers enhanced guidelines for the preparation, presentation and disclosure of pro forma financial information, smaller reporting companies may wish to consider these items.

Note 3 to §210.8: Financial statements for a subsidiary of a smaller reporting company that issues securities guaranteed by the smaller reporting company or guarantees securities issued by the smaller reporting company must be presented as required by §210.3-10, except that the periods presented are those required by §210.8-02.

Note 4 to §210.8: Financial statements for a smaller reporting company's affiliates whose securities constitute a substantial portion of the collateral for any class of securities registered or being registered must be presented as required by §210.3-16, except that the periods presented are those required by §210.8-02.

Note 5 to §210.8: The Commission, where consistent with the protection of investors, may permit the omission of one or more of the financial statements or the substitution of appropriate statements of comparable character. The Commission by informal written notice may require the filing of other financial statements where necessary or appropriate.

Note 6 to §210.8: Section 210.4-01(a)(3) shall apply to the preparation of financial statements of smaller reporting companies.

§210.8-02   Annual financial statements.

Smaller reporting companies shall file an audited balance sheet as of the end of each of the most recent two fiscal years, or as of a date within 135 days if the issuer has existed for a period of less than one fiscal year, and audited statements of income, cash flows and changes in stockholders' equity for each of the two fiscal years preceding the date of the most recent audited balance sheet (or such shorter period as the registrant has been in business).

§210.8-03 Interim financial statements.

Interim financial statements may be unaudited; however, before filing, interim financial statements included in quarterly reports on Form 10-Q (§249.308(a) of this chapter) must be reviewed by an independent public accountant using professional standards and procedures for conducting such reviews, as established by generally accepted auditing standards, as may be modified or supplemented by the Commission. If, in any filing, the issuer states that interim financial statements have been reviewed by an independent public accountant, a report of the accountant on the review must be filed with the interim financial statements. Interim financial statements shall include a balance sheet as of the end of the issuer's most recent fiscal quarter, a balance sheet as of the end of the preceding fiscal year, and income statements and statements of cash flows for the interim period up to the date of such balance sheet and the comparable period of the preceding fiscal year.

(a) Condensed format. Interim financial statements may be condensed as follows:

(1) Balance sheets should include separate captions for each balance sheet component presented in the annual financial statements that represents 10% or more of total assets. Cash and retained earnings should be presented regardless of relative significance to total assets. Registrants that present a classified balance sheet in their annual financial statements should present totals for current assets and current liabilities.

(2) Income statements should include net sales or gross revenue, each cost and expense category presented in the annual financial statements that exceeds 20% of sales or gross revenues, provision for income taxes, discontinued operations, extraordinary items and cumulative effects of changes in accounting principles or practices. (Financial institutions should substitute net interest income for sales for purposes of determining items to be disclosed.) Dividends per share should be presented.

(3) Cash flow statements should include cash flows from operating, investing and financing activities as well as cash at the beginning and end of each period and the increase or decrease in such balance.

(4) Additional line items may be presented to facilitate the usefulness of the interim financial statements, including their comparability with annual financial statements.

(b) Disclosure required and additional instructions as to content—(1) Footnotes. Footnote and other disclosures should be provided as needed for fair presentation and to ensure that the financial statements are not misleading.

(2) Material subsequent events and contingencies. Disclosure must be provided of material subsequent events and material contingencies notwithstanding disclosure in the annual financial statements.

(3) Significant equity investees. Sales, gross profit, net income (loss) from continuing operations, net income, and net income attributable to the investee must be disclosed for equity investees that constitute 20 percent or more of a registrant's consolidated assets, equity or income from continuing operations attributable to the registrant.

(4) Significant dispositions and business combinations. If a significant disposition or business combination has occurred during the most recent interim period and the transaction required the filing of a Form 8-K (§249.308 of this chapter), pro forma data must be presented that reflects revenue, income from continuing operations, net income, net income attributable to the registrant and income per share for the current interim period and the corresponding interim period of the preceding fiscal year as though the transaction occurred at the beginning of the periods.

(5) Material accounting changes. Disclosure must be provided of the date and reasons for any material accounting change. The registrant's independent accountant must provide a letter in the first Form 10-Q (§249.308a of this chapter) filed after the change indicating whether or not the change is to a preferable method. Disclosure must be provided of any retroactive change to prior period financial statements, including the effect of any such change on income and income per share.

(6) Development stage companies. A registrant in the development stage must provide cumulative financial information from inception.

Instruction 1 to §210.8-03: Where Article 8 is applicable to a Form 10-Q and the interim period is more than one quarter, income statements must also be provided for the most recent interim quarter and the comparable quarter of the preceding fiscal year.

Instruction 2 to §210.8-03: Interim financial statements must include all adjustments that, in the opinion of management, are necessary in order to make the financial statements not misleading. An affirmative statement that the financial statements have been so adjusted must be included with the interim financial statements.

[73 FR 953, Jan. 4, 2008, as amended at 74 FR 18615, Apr. 23, 2009]

§210.8-04 Financial statements of businesses acquired or to be acquired.
(a) If a business combination has occurred or is probable, financial statements of the business acquired or to be acquired shall be furnished for the periods specified in paragraph (c) of this section:

(1) This encompasses the purchase of an interest in a business accounted for by the equity method.

(2) Acquisitions of a group of related businesses that are probable or that have occurred subsequent to the latest fiscal year end for which audited financial statements of the issuer have been filed shall be treated as if they are a single business combination for purposes of this

117

section. The required financial statements of related businesses may be presented on a combined basis for any periods they are under common control or management. A group of businesses is deemed to be related if:

(i) They are under common control or management;

(ii) The acquisition of one business is conditioned on the acquisition of each other business; or

(iii) Each acquisition is conditioned on a single common event.

(3) Annual financial statements required by this rule shall be audited. The form and content of the financial statements shall be in accordance with §§210.8-02 and 8-03.

(b) The periods for which financial statements are to be presented are determined by comparison of the most recent annual financial statements of the business acquired or to be acquired and the smaller reporting company's most recent annual financial statements filed at or before the date of acquisition to evaluate each of the following conditions:

(1) Compare the smaller reporting company's investments in and advances to the acquiree to the total consolidated assets of the smaller reporting company as of the end of the most recently completed fiscal year.

(2) Compare the smaller reporting company's proportionate share of the total assets (after intercompany eliminations) of the acquiree to the total consolidated assets of the smaller reporting company as of the end of the most recently completed fiscal year.

(3) Compare the smaller reporting company's equity in the income from continuing operations before income taxes, extraordinary items and cumulative effect of a change in accounting principles of the acquiree exclusive of amounts attributable to any noncontrolling interests to such consolidated income of the smaller reporting company for the most recently completed fiscal year.

Computational note to §210.8-04(b): For purposes of making the prescribed income test the following guidance should be applied: If income of the smaller reporting company and its subsidiaries consolidated exclusive of amounts attributable to any noncontrolling interests for the most recent fiscal year is at least 10 percent lower than the average of the income for the last five fiscal years, such average income should be substituted for purposes of the computation. Any loss years should be omitted for purposes of computing average income.

(c)(1) If none of the conditions specified in paragraph (b) of this section exceeds 20%, financial statements are not required. If any of the conditions exceed 20%, but none exceeds 40%, financial statements shall be furnished for the most recent fiscal year and any interim periods specified in §210.8-03. If any of the conditions exceed 40%, financial statements shall be furnished for the two most recent fiscal years and any interim periods specified in §210.8-03.

(2) The separate audited balance sheet of the acquired business is not required when the smaller reporting company's most recent audited balance sheet filed is for a date after the acquisition was consummated.

(3) If the aggregate impact of individually insignificant businesses acquired since the date of the most recent audited balance sheet filed for the registrant exceeds 50%, financial statements covering at least the substantial majority of the businesses acquired shall be furnished. Such financial statements shall be for the most recent fiscal year and any interim periods specified in §210.8-03.

(4) Registration statements not subject to the provisions of §230.419 of this chapter (Regulation C) and proxy statements need not include separate financial statements of the acquired or to be acquired business if it does not meet or exceed any of the conditions specified in paragraph (b) of this section at the 50 percent level, and either:

(i) The consummation of the acquisition has not yet occurred; or

(ii) The effective date of the registration statement, or mailing date in the case of a proxy statement, is no more than 74 days after consummation of the business combination, and the financial statements have not been filed previously by the registrant.

(5) An issuer that omits from its initial registration statement financial statements of a recently consummated business combination pursuant to paragraph (c)(4) of this section shall furnish those financial statements and any pro forma information specified by §210.8-05 under cover of Form 8-K (§249.308 of this chapter) no later than 75 days after consummation of the acquisition.

(d) If the smaller reporting company made a significant business acquisition after the latest fiscal year end and filed a report on Form 8-K, which included audited financial statements of such acquired business for the periods required by paragraph (c) of this section and the pro forma financial information required by §210.8-05, the determination of significance may be made by using pro forma amounts for the latest fiscal year in the report on Form 8-K rather than by using the historical amounts of the registrant. The tests may not be made by "annualizing" data.

(e) If the business acquired or to be acquired is a foreign business, financial statements of the business meeting the requirements of Item 17 of Form 20-F (§249.220f of this chapter) will satisfy this section.

[73 FR 953, Jan. 4, 2008, as amended at 74 FR 18616, Apr. 23, 2009]

§210.8-05 Pro forma financial information.

(a) Pro forma information showing the effects of the acquisition shall be furnished if financial statements of a business acquired or to be acquired are presented.

(b) Pro forma statements should be condensed, in columnar form showing pro forma adjustments and results, and should include the following:

(1) If the transaction was consummated during the most recent fiscal year or subsequent interim period, pro forma statements of income reflecting the combined operations of the entities for the latest fiscal year and interim period, if any; or

(2) If consummation of the transaction has occurred or is probable after the date of the most recent balance sheet required by §210.8-02 or §210.8-03, a pro forma balance sheet giving effect to the combination as of the date of the most recent balance sheet. For a purchase, pro forma statements of income reflecting the combined operations of the entities for the latest fiscal year and interim period, if any, are required.

§210.8-06 Real estate operations acquired or to be acquired.

If, during the period for which income statements are required, the smaller reporting company has acquired one or more properties that in the aggregate are significant, or since the date of the latest balance sheet required by §210.8-02 or §210.8-03, has acquired or proposes to acquire one or more properties that in the aggregate are significant, the following shall be furnished with respect to such properties:

(a) Audited income statements (not including earnings per unit) for the two most recent years, which shall exclude items not comparable to the proposed future operations of the property such as mortgage interest, leasehold rental, depreciation, corporate expenses and federal and state income taxes; Provided, however, that such audited statements need be presented for only the most recent fiscal year if:

(1) The property is not acquired from a related party;

(2) Material factors considered by the smaller reporting company in assessing the property are described with specificity in the registration statement with regard to the property, including source of revenue (including, but not limited to, competition in the rental market, comparative rents, occupancy rates) and expenses (including but not limited to, utilities, ad valorem tax rates, maintenance expenses, and capital improvements anticipated); and

(3) The smaller reporting company indicates that, after reasonable inquiry, it is not aware of any material factors relating to the specific property other than those discussed in response to paragraph (a)(2) of this section that would cause the reported financial information not to be necessarily indicative of future operating results.

(b) If the property will be operated by the smaller reporting company, a statement shall be furnished showing the estimated taxable operating results of the smaller reporting company based on the most recent twelve-month period, including such adjustments as can be factually supported. If the property will be acquired subject to a net lease, the estimated taxable operating results shall be based on the rent to be paid for the first year of the lease. In either case, the estimated amount of cash to be made available by operations shall be shown. Disclosure must be provided of the principal assumptions that have been made in preparing the statements of estimated taxable operating results and cash to be made available by operations.

(c) If appropriate under the circumstances, a table should be provided that shows, for a limited number of years, the estimated cash distribution per unit, indicating the portion reportable as taxable income and the portion representing a return of capital with an explanation of annual variations, if any. If taxable net income per unit will be greater than the cash available for distribution per unit, that fact and the approximate year of occurrence shall be stated, if significant.

§210.8-07 Limited partnerships.
(a) Smaller reporting companies that are limited partnerships must provide the balance sheets of the general partners as described in paragraphs (b) through (d) of this section.

(b) Where a general partner is a corporation, the audited balance sheet of the corporation as of the end of its most recently completed fiscal year must be filed. Receivables, other than trade receivables, from affiliates of the general partner should be deducted from shareholders' equity of the general partner. Where an affiliate has committed itself to increase or maintain the general partner's capital, the audited balance sheet of such affiliate must also be presented.

(c) Where a general partner is a partnership, there shall be filed an audited balance sheet of such partnership as of the end of its most recently completed fiscal year.

(d) Where the general partner is a natural person, there shall be filed, as supplemental information, a balance sheet of such natural person as of a recent date. Such balance sheet need not be audited. The assets and liabilities should be carried at estimated fair market value, with provisions for estimated income taxes on unrealized gains. The net worth of such general partner(s), based on such balance sheet(s), singly or in the aggregate, shall be disclosed in the registration statement.

§210.8-08 Age of financial statements.
At the date of filing, financial statements included in filings other than filings on Form 10-K must be not less current than the financial statements that would be required in Forms 10-K and 10-Q if such reports were required to be filed. If required financial statements are as of a date 135 days or more before the date a registration statement becomes effective or proxy material is expected to be mailed, the financial statements shall be updated to include financial statements for an interim period ending within 135 days of the effective or expected mailing date. Interim financial statements must be prepared and presented in accordance with paragraph (b) of this section.

(a) When the anticipated effective or mailing date falls within 45 days after the end of the fiscal year, the filing may include financial statements only as current as of the end of the third fiscal quarter; Provided, however, that if the audited financial statements for the recently completed fiscal year are available or become available before effectiveness or mailing, they must be included in the filing; and

(b) If the effective date or anticipated mailing date falls after 45 days but within 90 days of the end of the smaller reporting company's fiscal year, the smaller reporting company is not required to provide the audited financial statements for such year end provided that the following conditions are met:

(1) If the smaller reporting company is a reporting company, all reports due must have been filed;

(2) For the most recent fiscal year for which audited financial statements are not yet available, the smaller reporting company reasonably and in good faith expects to report income from continuing operations attributable to the registrant before taxes; and

(3) For at least one of the two fiscal years immediately preceding the most recent fiscal year the smaller reporting company reported income from continuing operations attributable to the registrant before taxes.

[73 FR 953, Jan. 4, 2008, as amended at 74 FR 18616, Apr. 23, 2009]

Bank Holding Companies
Source: Sections 210.9-01 through 210.9-07 appear at 48 FR 11107, Mar. 16, 1983, unless otherwise noted.

§210.9-01 Application of §§210.9-01 to 210.9-07
This article is applicable to consolidated financial statements filed for bank holding companies and to any financial statements of banks that are included in filings with the Commission.

§210.9-02 General requirement.
The requirements of the general rules in §§210.1 to 210.4 (Articles 1, 2, 3, 3A and 4) should be complied with where applicable.

§210.9-03 Balance sheets.
The purpose of this rule is to indicate the various items which, if applicable, should appear on the face of the balance sheets or in the notes thereto.

Assets
1. Cash and due from banks. The amounts in this caption should include all noninterest bearing deposits with other banks.

(a) Any withdrawal and usage restrictions (including requirements of the Federal Reserve to maintain certain average reserve balances) or compensating balance requirements should be disclosed (see §210.5-02-1).

2. Interest-bearing deposits in other banks.

3. Federal funds sold and securities purchased under resale agreements of similar arrangements. These amounts should be presented gross and not netted against Federal funds purchased and securities sold under agreement to repurchase as reported in Caption 13.

4. Trading account assets. Include securities or any other investments held for trading purposes only.

5. Other short-term investments.

6. Investment securities Include securities held for investment only. Disclose the aggregate book value of investment securities; show on the balance sheet the aggregate market value at the balance sheet date. The aggregate amounts should include securities pledged, loaned or sold under repurchase agreements and similar arrangements; borrowed securities and securities purchased under resale agreements or similar arrangements should be excluded.

(a) Disclose in a note the carrying value and market value of securities of (1) the U.S. Treasury and other U.S. Government agencies and corporations; (2) states of the U.S. and political subdivisions; and (3) other securities.

7. Loans. Disclose separately (1) total loans, (2) the related allowance for losses and (3) unearned income.

(a) Disclose on the balance sheet or in a note the amount of total loans in each of the following categories:

(1) Commercial, financial and agricultural

(2) Real estate—construction

(3) Real estate—mortgage

(4) Installment loans to individuals

(5) Lease financing

(6) Foreign

(7) Other (State separately any other loan category regardless of relative size if necessary to reflect any unusual risk concentration).

(b) A series of categories other than those specified in (a) above may be used to present details of loans if considered a more appropriate presentation.

(c) The amount of foreign loans must be presented if the disclosures provided by §210.9-05 are required.

(d) For each period for which an income statement is required, furnish in a note a statement of changes in the allowance for loan losses showing the balances at beginning and end of the period provision charged to income, recoveries of amounts charged off and losses charged to the allowance.

(e)(1)(i) As of each balance sheet date, disclose in a note the aggregate dollar amount of loans (exclusive of loans to any such persons which in the aggregate do not exceed $60,000 during the latest year) made by the registrant or any of its subsidiaries to directors, executive officers, or principal holders of equity securities (§210.1-02) of the registrant or any of its significant subsidiaries (§210.1-02), or to any associate of such persons. For the latest fiscal year, an analysis of activity with respect to such aggregate loans to related parties should be provided. The analysis should include the aggregate amount at the beginning of the period, new loans, repayments, and other changes. (Other changes, if significant, should be explained.)

(ii) This disclosure need not be furnished when the aggregate amount of such loans at the balance sheet date (or with respect to the latest fiscal year, the maximum amount outstanding during the period) does not exceed 5 percent of stockholders equity at the balance sheet date.

(2) If a significant portion of the aggregate amount of loans outstanding at the end of the fiscal year disclosed pursuant to (e)(1)(i) above relates to loans which are disclosed as nonaccrual, past due, restructured or potential problems (see Item III.C. 1. or 2. of Industry Guide 3, Statistical Disclosure by Bank Holding Companies), so state and disclose the aggregate amounts of such loans along with such other information necessary to an understanding of the effects of the transactions on the financial statements.

(3) Notwithstanding the aggregate disclosure called for by (e)(1) above, if any loans were not made in the ordinary course of business during any period for which an income statement is required to be filed, provide an appropriate description of each such loan (see §210.4-08(L)(3)).

(4) Definition of terms. For purposes of this rule, the following definitions shall apply:

Associate means (i) a corporation, venture or organization of which such person is a general partner or is, directly or indirectly, the beneficial owner of 10 percent or more of any class of equity securities; (ii) any trust or other estate in which such person has a substantial beneficial interest or for which such person serves as trustee or in a similar capacity and (iii) any member of the immediate family of any of the foregoing persons.

Executive officers means the president, any vice president in charge of a principal business unit, division or function (such as loans, investments, operations, administration or finance), and any other officer or person who performs similar policymaking functions.

Immediate Family means such person's spouse; parents; children; siblings; mothers and fathers-in-law; sons and daughters-in-law; and brothers and sisters-in-law.

Ordinary course of business means those loans which were made on substantially the same terms, including interest rate and collateral, as those prevailing at the same time for comparable transactions with unrelated persons and did not involve more than the normal risk of collectibility or present other unfavorable features.

8. Premises and equipment.

9. Due from customers on acceptances. Include amounts receivable from customers on unmatured drafts and bills of exchange that have been accepted by a bank subsidiary or by other banks for the account of a subsidiary and that are outstanding—that is, not held by a subsidiary bank, on the reporting date. (If held by a bank subsidiary, they should be reported as "loans" under §210.9-03.7.)

10. Other assets. Disclose separately on the balance sheet or in a note thereto any of the following assets or any other asset the amount of which exceeds thirty percent of stockholders equity. The remaining assets may be shown as one amount.

(1) Excess of cost over tangible and identifiable intangible assets acquired (net of amortization).

(2) Other intangible assets (net of amortization).

(3) Investments in and indebtness of affiliates and other persons.

(4) Other real estates.

(a) Disclose in a note the basis at which other real estate is carried. An reduction to fair market value from the carrying value of the related loan at the time of acquisition shall be accounted for as a loan loss. Any allowance for losses on other real estate which has been established subsequent to acquisition should be deducted from other real estate. For each period for which an income statement is required, disclosures should be made in a note as to the changes in the allowances, including balance at beginning and end of period, provision charged to income, and losses charged to the allowance.

11. Total assets.

Liabilities and Stockholders' Equity
Liabilities
12. Deposits. Disclose separately the amounts of noninterest bearing deposits and interest bearing deposits.

(a) The amount of noninterest bearing deposits and interest bearing deposits in foreign banking offices must be presented if the disclosure provided by §210.0-05 are required.

13. Short-term borrowing. Disclosure separately on the balance sheet or in a note, amounts payable for (1) Federal funds purchased and securities sold under agreements to repurchase; (2) commercial paper, and (3) other short-term borrowings.

(a) Disclose any unused lines of credit for short-term financing: (§210.5-02.19(b)).

14. Bank acceptances outstanding. Disclose the aggregate of unmatured drafts and bills of exchange accepted by a bank subsidiary, or by some other bank as its agent, less the amount of such acceptances acquired by the bank subsidiary through discount or purchase.

15. Other liabilities. Disclose separately on the balance sheet or in a note any of the following liabilities or any other items which are individually in excess of thirty percent of stockholders' equity (except that amounts in excess of 5 percent of stockholders' equity should be disclosed with respect to item (4)). The remaining items may be shown as one amount.

(1) Income taxes payable.

(2) Deferred income taxes.

(3) Indebtedness to affiliates and other persons the investments in which are accounted for by the equity method.

(4) Indebtedness to directors, executive officers, and principal holders of equity securities of the registrant or any of its significant subsidiaries (the guidance in §210.9-03.7(e) shall be used to identify related parties for purposes of this disclosure).

(5) Accounts payable and accrued expenses.

16. Long-term debt. Disclose in a note the information required by §210.5-02.22.

17. Commitments and contingent liabilities.

Redeemable Preferred Stocks
18. Preferred stocks subject to mandatory redemption requirements or whose redemption is outside the control of the issuer. See §210.5-02.27.

Non-redeemable Preferred Stocks
19. Preferred stocks which are not redeemable or are redeemable solely at the option of the issuer. See §210.5-02.28.

Common Stocks
20. Common stocks. See §210.5-02.29.

Other Stockholders' Equity
21. Other stockholders' equity. See §210.5-02.30.

Noncontrolling Interests

22. Noncontrolling interests in consolidated subsidiaries. The disclosure requirements of §210.5-02.31 shall be followed.

23. Total liabilities and equity.

[48 FR 11107, Mar. 16, 1983, as amended at 48 FR 37612, Aug. 19, 1983; 50 FR 25215, June 18, 1985; 74 FR 18616, Apr. 23, 2009]

§210.9-04 Income statements.

The purpose of this rule is to indicate the various items which, if applicable, should appear on the face of the income statement or in the notes thereto.

1. Interest and fees on loans. Include commitment and origination fees, late charges and current amortization of premium and accretion of discount on loans which are related to or are an adjustment of the loan interest rate.

2. Interest and dividends on investment securities. Disclosure separately (1) taxable interest income, (2) nontaxable interest income, and (3) dividends.

3. Trading account interest.

4. Other interest income.

5. Total interest income (total of lines 1 through 4).

6. Interest on deposits.

7. Interest on short-term borrowings.

8. Interest on long-term debt.

9. Total interest expense (total of lines 6 through 8).

10. Net interest income (line 5 minus line 9).

11. Provision for loan losses.

12. Net interest income after provision for loan losses.

13. Other income. Disclose separately any of the following amounts, or any other item of other income, which exceed one percent of the aggregate of total interest income and other income. The remaining amounts may be shown as one amount, except for investment securities gains or losses which shall be shown separately regardless of size.

(a) Commissions and fees and fiduciary activities.

(b) Commissions, broker's fees and markups on securities underwriting and other securities activities.

(c) Insurance commissions, fees and premiums.

(d) Fees for other customer services.

(e) Profit or loss on transactions in securities in dealer trading account.

(f) Equity in earnings of unconsolidated subsidiaries and 50 percent or less owned persons.

(g) Gains or losses on disposition of equity in securities of subsidiaries or 50 percent or less owned persons.

(h) Investment securities gains or losses. The method followed in determining the cost of investments sold (e.g., "average cost," "first-in, first-out," or "identified certificate) and related income taxes shall be disclosed.

14. Other expenses. Disclose separately any of the following amounts, or any other item of other expense, which exceed one percent of the aggregate of total interest income and other income. The remaining amounts may be shown as one amount.

(a) Salaries and employee benefits.

(b) Net occupancy expense of premises.

(c) Goodwill amortization.

(d) Net cost of operation of other real estate (including provisions for real estate losses, rental income and gains and losses on sales of real estate).

15. Income or loss before income tax expense.

16. Income tax expense. The information required by §210.4-08(h) should be disclosed.

17. Income or loss before extraordinary items and cumulative effects of changes in accounting principles.

18. Extraordinary items, less applicable tax.

19. Cumulative effects of changes in accounting principles.

20. Net income or loss.

21. Net income attributable to the noncontrolling interest.

22. Net income attributable to the controlling interest.

23. Earnings per share data.

[48 FR 11107, Mar. 16, 1983, as amended at 50 FR 25215, June 18, 1985; 74 FR 18616, Apr. 23, 2009]

§210.9-05   Foreign activities.

(a) General requirement. Separate disclosure concerning foreign activities shall be made for each period in which either (1) assets, or (2) revenue, or (3) income (loss) before income tax expense, or (4) net income (loss), each as associated with foreign activities, exceeded ten percent of the corresponding amount in the related financial statements.

(b) Disclosures. (1) Disclose total identifiable assets (net of valuation allowances) associated with foreign activities.

(2) For each period for which an income statement is filed, state the amount of revenue, income (loss) before taxes, and net income (loss) associated with foreign activities. Disclose significant estimates and assumptions (including those related to the cost of capital) used in allocating revenue and expenses to foreign activities; describe the nature and effects of any changes in such estimates and assumptions which have a significant impact on interperiod comparability.

(3) The information in paragraph (b) (1) and (2) of this section shall be presented separately for each significant geographic area and in the aggregate for all other geographic areas not deemed significant.

(c) Definitions. (1) Foreign activities include loans and other revenues producing assets and transactions in which the debtor or customer, whether an affiliated or unaffiliated person, is domiciled outside the United States.

(2) The term revenue includes the total of the amount reported at §§210.9-04.5 and 210.9-04.13.

(3) A significant geographic area is one in which assets or revenue or income before income tax or net income exceed 10 percent of the comparable amount as reported in the financial statements.

§210.9-06   Condensed financial information of registrant.

The information prescribed by §210.12-04 shall be presented in a note to the financial statements when the restricted net assets (§210.4-08(e)(3)) of consolidated subsidiaries exceed 25 percent of consolidated net assets as of the end of the most recently completed fiscal year. The investment in and indebtedness of and to bank subsidiaries shall be stated separately in the condensed balance sheet from amounts for other subsidiaries; the amount of cash dividends paid to the registrant for each of the last three years by bank subsidiaries shall be stated separately in the condensed income statement from amounts for other subsidiaries. For purposes of the above test, restricted net assets of consolidated subsidiaries shall mean that amount of the registrant's proportionate share of net assets of consolidated subsidiaries (after intercompany eliminations) which as of the end of the most recent fiscal year may not be transferred to the parent company by subsidiaries in the form of loans, advances or cash dividends without the consent of a third party (i.e., lender, regulatory agency, foreign government, etc.). Where restrictions on the amount of funds which may be loaned or advanced differ from the amount restricted as to transfer in the form of cash dividends, the amount least restrictive to the subsidiary shall be used. Redeemable preferred stocks (§210.5-02.27) and noncontrolling interests shall be deducted in computing net assets for purposes of this test.

[48 FR 11107, Mar. 16, 1983, as amended at 74 FR 18616, Apr. 23, 2009]

§210.9-07   [Reserved]

Interim Financial Statements

§210.10-01   Interim financial statements.
(a) Condensed statements. Interim financial statements shall follow the general form and content of presentation prescribed by the other sections of this Regulation with the following exceptions:

(1) Interim financial statements required by this rule need only be provided as to the registrant and its subsidiaries consolidated and may be unaudited. Separate statements of other entities which may otherwise be required by this regulation may be omitted.

(2) Interim balance sheets shall include only major captions (i.e., numbered captions) prescribed by the applicable sections of this Regulation with the exception of inventories. Data as to raw materials, work in process and finished goods inventories shall be included either on the face of the balance sheet or in the notes to the financial statements, if applicable. Where any major balance sheet caption is less than 10% of total assets, and the amount in the caption has not increased or decreased by more than 25% since the end of the preceding fiscal year, the caption may be combined with others.

(3) Interim statements of income shall also include major captions prescribed by the applicable sections of this Regulation. When any major income statement caption is less than 15% of average net income for the most recent three fiscal years and the amount in the caption has not increased or decreased by more than 20% as compared to the corresponding interim period of the preceding fiscal year, the caption may be combined with others. In calculating average net income, loss years should be excluded. If losses were incurred in each of the most recent three years, the average loss shall be used for purposes of this test. Notwithstanding these tests, §210.4-02 applies and de minimis amounts therefore need not be shown separately, except that registrants reporting under §210.9 shall show investment securities gains or losses separately regardless of size.

(4) The statement of cash flows may be abbreviated starting with a single figure of net cash flows from operating activities and showing cash changes from investing and financing activities individually only when they exceed 10% of the average of net cash flows from operating activities for the most recent three years. Notwithstanding this test, §210.4-02 applies and de minimis amounts therefore need not be shown separately.

(5) The interim financial information shall include disclosures either on the face of the financial statements or in accompanying footnotes sufficient so as to make the interim information presented not misleading. Registrants may presume that users of the interim financial information have read or have access to the audited financial statements for the preceding fiscal year and that the adequacy of additional disclosure needed for a fair presentation, except in regard to material contingencies, may be determined in that context. Accordingly, footnote disclosure which would substantially duplicate the disclosure contained in the most recent annual report to security holders or latest audited financial statements, such as a statement of significant accounting policies and practices, details of accounts which have not changed significantly in amount or composition since the end of the most recently completed fiscal year, and detailed disclosures prescribed by Rule 4-08 of this Regulation, may be omitted. However, disclosure shall be provided where events subsequent to the end of the most recent fiscal year have occurred which have a material impact on the registrant. Disclosures should encompass for example, significant changes since the end of the most recently completed fiscal year in such items as: accounting principles and practices; estimates inherent in the preparation of financial statements; status of long-term contracts; capitalization including significant new borrowings or modification of existing financing arrangements; and the reporting entity resulting from business combinations or dispositions. Notwithstanding the above, where material contingencies exist, disclosure of such matters shall be provided even though a significant change since year end may not have occurred.

(6) Detailed schedules otherwise required by this Regulation may be omitted for purposes of preparing interim financial statements.

(7) In addition to the financial statements required by paragraphs (a) (2), (3) and (4) of this section, registrants in the development stage shall provide the cumulative financial statements (condensed to the same degree as allowed in this paragraph) and disclosures required by FASB ASC Topic 915, Development Stage Entities, to the date of the latest balance sheet presented.

(b) Other instructions as to content. The following additional instructions shall be applicable for purposes of preparing interim financial statements:

(1) Summarized income statement information shall be given separately as to each subsidiary not consolidated or 50 percent or less owned persons or as to each group of such subsidiaries or fifty percent or less owned persons for which separate individual or group statements would otherwise be required for annual periods. Such summarized information, however, need not be furnished for any such unconsolidated subsidiary or person which would not be required pursuant to Rule 13a-13 or 15d-13 to file quarterly financial information with the Commission if it were a registrant.

(2) If appropriate, the income statement shall show earnings per share and dividends declared per share applicable to common stock. The basis of the earnings per share computation shall be stated together with the number of shares used in the computation. In addition, see Item 601(b)(11) of Regulation S-K, (17 CFR 229.601(b)(11)).

(3) If, during the most recent interim period presented, the registrant or any of its consolidated subsidiaries entered into a combination between entities under common control, the interim financial statements for both the current year and the preceding year shall reflect the combined results of the combined businesses. Supplemental disclosure of the separate results of the combined entities for periods prior to the combination shall be given, with appropriate explanations.

(4) Where a material business combination has occurred during the current fiscal year, pro forma disclosure shall be made of the results of operations for the current year up to the date of the most recent interim balance sheet provided (and for the corresponding period in the preceding year) as though the companies had combined at the beginning of the period being reported on. This pro forma information shall, at a minimum, show revenue, income before extraordinary items and the cumulative effect of accounting changes, including such income on a per share basis, net income, net income attributable to the registrant, and net income per share.

(5) Where the registrant has reported a discontinued operation (as required by FASB ASC Subtopic 205-20, Presentation of Financial Statements—Discontinued Operations) during any of the periods covered by the interim financial statements, the effect thereof on revenues and net income—total and per share—for all periods shall be disclosed.

(6) In addition to meeting the reporting requirements specified by existing standards for accounting changes, the registrant shall state the date of any material accounting change and the reasons for making it. In addition, for filings on Form 10-Q, a letter from the registrant's independent accountant shall be filed as an exhibit (in accordance with the provisions of Item 601 of Regulation S-K, 17 CFR 229.601) in the first Form 10-Q after the date of an accounting change indicating whether or not the change is to an alternative principle which, in the accountant's judgment, is preferable under the circumstances; except that no letter from the accountant need be filed when the change is made in response to a standard adopted by the Financial Accounting Standards Board that requires such change.

(7) Any material retroactive prior period adjustment made during any period convered by the interim financial statements shall be disclosed, together with the effect thereof upon net income—total and per share—of any prior period included and upon the balance of retained earnings. If results of operations for any period presented have been adjusted retroactively by such an item subsequent to the initial reporting of such period, similar disclosure of the effect of the change shall be made.

(8) Any unaudited interim financial statements furnished shall reflect all adjustments which are, in the opinion of management, necessary to a fair statement of the results for the interim periods presented. A statement to that effect shall be included. Such adjustments shall include, for example, appropriate estimated provisions for bonus and profit sharing arrangements normally

determined or settled at year-end. If all such adjustments are of a normal recurring nature, a statement to that effect shall be made; otherwise, there shall be furnished information describing in appropriate detail the nature and amount of any adjustments other than normal recurring adjustments entering into the determination of the results shown.

(c) Periods to be covered. The periods for which interim financial statements are to be provided in registration statements are prescribed elsewhere in this Regulation (see §§210.3-01 and 3-02). For filings on Form 10-Q, financial statements shall be provided as set forth in this paragraph (c):

(1) An interim balance sheet as of the end of the most recent fiscal quarter and a balance sheet as of the end of the preceding fiscal year shall be provided. The balance sheet as of the end of the preceding fiscal year may be condensed to the same degree as the interim balance sheet provided. An interim balance sheet as of the end of the corresponding fiscal quarter of the preceding fiscal year need not be provided unless necessary for an understanding of the impact of seasonal fluctuations on the registrant's financial condition.

(2) Interim statements of income shall be provided for the most recent fiscal quarter, for the period between the end of the preceding fiscal year and the end of the most recent fiscal quarter, and for the corresponding periods of the preceding fiscal year. Such statements may also be presented for the cumulative twelve month period ended during the most recent fiscal quarter and for the corresponding preceding period.

(3) Interim statements of cash flows shall be provided for the period between the end of the preceding fiscal year and the end of the most recent fiscal quarter, and for the corresponding period of the preceding fiscal year. Such statements may also be presented for the cumulative twelve month period ended during the most recent fiscal quarter and for the corresponding preceding period.

(4) Registrants engaged in seasonal production and sale of a single-crop agricultural commodity may provide interim statements of income and cash flows for the twelve month period ended during the most recent fiscal quarter and for the corresponding preceding period in lieu of the year-to-date statements specified in (2) and (3) above.

(d) Interim review by independent public accountant. Prior to filing, interim financial statements included in quarterly reports on Form 10-Q (17 CFR 249.308(a)) must be reviewed by an independent public accountant using professional standards and procedures for conducting such reviews, as established by generally accepted auditing standards, as may be modified or supplemented by the Commission. If, in any filing, the company states that interim financial statements have been reviewed by an independent public accountant, a report of the accountant on the review must be filed with the interim financial statements.

(e) Filing of other interim financial information in certain cases. The Commission may, upon the informal written request of the registrant, and where consistent with the protection of investors, permit the omission of any of the interim financial information herein required or the filing in substitution thereof of appropriate information of comparable character. The Commission may also by informal written notice require the filing of other information in addition to, or in substitution for, the interim information herein required in any case where such information is necessary or appropriate for an adequate presentation of the financial condition of any person for which interim financial information is required, or whose financial information is otherwise necessary for the protection of investors.

[46 FR 12489, Feb. 17, 1981, as amended at 50 FR 25215, June 18, 1985; 50 FR 49533, Dec. 3, 1985; 57 FR 45293, Oct. 1, 1992; 64 FR 73401, Dec. 30, 1999; 73 FR 956, Jan. 4, 2008; 74 FR 18616, Apr. 23, 2009; 76 FR 50120, Aug. 12, 2011]

Pro Forma Financial Information
Source: Sections 210.11-01 through 210.11-03 appear at 47 FR 29837, July 9, 1982, unless otherwise noted.

§210.11-01 Presentation requirements.
(a) Pro forma financial information shall be furnished when any of the following conditions exist:

(1) During the most recent fiscal year or subsequent interim period for which a balance sheet is required by §210.3-01, a significant business combination has occurred (for purposes of these rules, this encompasses the acquisition of an interest in a business accounted for by the equity method);

(2) After the date of the most recent balance sheet filed pursuant to §210.3-01, consummation of a significant business combination or a combination of entities under common control has occurred or is probable;

(3) Securities being registered by the registrant are to be offered to the security holders of a significant business to be acquired or the proceeds from the offered securities will be applied directly or indirectly to the purchase of a specific significant business;

(4) The disposition of a significant portion of a business either by sale, abandonment or distribution to shareholders by means of a spin-off, split-up or split-off has occurred or is probable and such disposition is not fully reflected in the financial statements of the registrant included in the filing;

(5) During the most recent fiscal year or subsequent interim period for which a balance sheet is required by §210.3-01, the registrant has acquired one or more real estate operations or properties which in the aggregate are significant, or since the date of the most recent balance sheet filed pursuant to that section the registrant has acquired or proposes to acquire one or more operations or properties which in the aggregate are significant.

(6) Pro forma financial information required by §229.914 is required to be provided in connection with a roll-up transaction as defined in §229.901(c).

(7) The registrant previously was a part of another entity and such presentation is necessary to reflect operations and financial position of the registrant as an autonomous entity; or

(8) Consummation of other events or transactions has occurred or is probable for which disclosure of pro forma financial information would be material to investors.

(b) A business combination or disposition of a business shall be considered significant if:

(1) A comparison of the most recent annual financial statements of the business acquired or to be acquired and the registrant's most recent annual consolidated financial statements filed at or prior to the date of acquisition indicates that the business would be a significant subsidiary pursuant to the conditions specified in §210.1-02(w), substituting 20 percent for 10 percent each place it appears therein; or

(2) The business to be disposed of meets the conditions of a significant subsidiary in §210.1-02(w).

(c) The pro forma effects of a business combination need not be presented pursuant to this section if separate financial statements of the acquired business are not included in the filing.

(d) For purposes of this rule, the term business should be evaluated in light of the facts and circumstances involved and whether there is sufficient continuity of the acquired entity's operations prior to and after the transactions so that disclosure of prior financial information is material to an understanding of future operations. A presumption exists that a separate entity, a subsidiary, or a division is a business. However, a lesser component of an entity may also constitute a business. Among the facts and circumstances which should be considered in evaluating whether an acquisition of a lesser component of an entity constitutes a business are the following:

(1) Whether the nature of the revenue-producing activity of the component will remain generally the same as before the transaction; or

(2) Whether any of the following attributes remain with the component after the transaction:

(i) Physical facilities,

(ii) Employee base,

(iii) Market distribution system,

(iv) Sales force,

(v) Customer base,

(vi) Operating rights,

(vii) Production techniques, or

(viii) Trade names.

(e) This rule does not apply to transactions between a parent company and its totally held subsidiary.

[47 FR 29837, July 9, 1982, as amended at 50 FR 49533, Dec. 3, 1985; 56 FR 57247, Nov. 8, 1991; 61 FR 54514, Oct. 18, 1996; 74 FR 18616, Apr. 23, 2009]

§210.11-02 Preparation requirements.

(a) Objective. Pro forma financial information should provide investors with information about the continuing impact of a particular transaction by showing how it might have affected historical financial statements if the transaction had been consummated at an earlier time. Such statements should assist investors in analyzing the future prospects of the registrant because they illustrate the possible scope of the change in the registrant's historical financial position and results of operations caused by the transaction.

(b) Form and content. (1) Pro forma financial information shall consist of a pro forma condensed balance sheet, pro forma condensed statements of income, and accompanying explanatory notes. In certain circumstances (i.e., where a limited number of pro forma adjustments are required and those adjustments are easily understood), a narrative description of the pro forma effects of the transaction may be furnished in lieu of the statements described herein.

(2) The pro forma financial information shall be accompanied by an introductory paragraph which briefly sets forth a description of (i) the transaction, (ii) the entities involved, and (iii) the periods for which the pro forma information is presented. In addition, an explanation of what the pro forma presentation shows shall be set forth.

(3) The pro forma condensed financial information need only include major captions (i.e., the numbered captions) prescribed by the applicable sections of this Regulation. Where any major balance sheet caption is less than 10 percent of total assets, the caption may be combined with others. When any major income statement caption is less than 15 percent of average net income attributable to the registrant for the most recent three fiscal years, the caption may be combined with others. In calculating average net income attributable to the registrant, loss years should be excluded unless losses were incurred in each of the most recent three years, in which case the average loss shall be used for purposes of this test. Notwithstanding these tests, de minimis amounts need not be shown separately.

(4) Pro forma statements shall ordinarily be in columnar form showing condensed historical statements, pro forma adjustments, and the pro forma results.

(5) The pro forma condensed income statement shall disclose income (loss) from continuing operations before nonrecurring charges or credits directly attributable to the transaction. Material

nonrecurring charges or credits and related tax effects which result directly from the transaction and which will be included in the income of the registrant within the 12 months succeeding the transaction shall be disclosed separately. It should be clearly indicated that such charges or credits were not considered in the pro forma condensed income statement. If the transaction for which pro forma financial information is presented relates to the disposition of a business, the pro forma results should give effect to the disposition and be presented under an appropriate caption.

(6) Pro forma adjustments related to the pro forma condensed income statement shall be computed assuming the transaction was consummated at the beginning of the fiscal year presented and shall include adjustments which give effect to events that are (i) directly attributable to the transaction, (ii) expected to have a continuing impact on the registrant, and (iii) factually supportable. Pro forma adjustments related to the pro forma condensed balance sheet shall be computed assuming the transaction was consummated at the end of the most recent period for which a balance sheet is required by §210.3-01 and shall include adjustments which give effect to events that are directly attributable to the transaction and factually supportable regardless of whether they have a continuing impact or are nonrecurring. All adjustments should be referenced to notes which clearly explain the assumptions involved.

(7) Historical primary and fully diluted per share data based on continuing operations (or net income if the registrant does not report either discontinued operations, extraordinary items, or the cumulative effects of accounting changes) for the registrant, and primary and fully diluted pro forma per share data based on continuing operations before nonrecurring charges or credits directly attributable to the transaction shall be presented on the face of the pro forma condensed income statement together with the number of shares used to compute such per share data. For transactions involving the issuance of securities, the number of shares used in the calculation of the pro forma per share data should be based on the weighted average number of shares outstanding during the period adjusted to give effect to shares subsequently issued or assumed to be issued had the particular transaction or event taken place at the beginning of the period presented. If a convertible security is being issued in the transaction, consideration should be given to the possible dilution of the pro forma per share data.

(8) If the transaction is structured in such a manner that significantly different results may occur, additional pro forma presentations shall be made which give effect to the range of possible results.

Instructions: 1. The historical statement of income used in the pro forma financial information shall not report operations of a segment that has been discontinued, extraordinary items, or the cumulative effects of accounting changes. If the historical statement of income includes such items, only the portion of the income statement through "income from continuing operations" (or the appropriate modification thereof) should be used in preparing pro forma results.

2. For a business combination, pro forma adjustments for the income statement shall include amortization, depreciation and other adjustments based on the allocated purchase price of net assets acquired. In some transactions, such as in financial institution acquisitions, the purchase adjustments may include significant discounts of the historical cost of the acquired assets to their

fair value at the acquisition date. When such adjustments will result in a significant effect on earnings (losses) in periods immediately subsequent to the acquisition which will be progressively eliminated over a relatively short period, the effect of the purchase adjustments on reported results of operations for each of the next five years should be disclosed in a note.

3. For a disposition transaction, the pro forma financial information shall begin with the historical financial statements of the existing entity and show the deletion of the business to be divested along with the pro forma adjustments necessary to arrive at the remainder of the existing entity. For example, pro forma adjustments would include adjustments of interest expense arising from revised debt structures and expenses which will be or have been incurred on behalf of the business to be divested such as advertising costs, executive salaries and other costs.

4. For entities which were previously a component of another entity, pro forma adjustments should include adjustments similar in nature to those referred to in Instruction 3 above. Adjustments may also be necessary when charges for corporate overhead, interest, or income taxes have been allocated to the entity on a basis other than one deemed reasonable by management.

5. Adjustments to reflect the acquisition of real estate operations or properties for the pro forma income statement shall include a depreciation charge based on the new accounting basis for the assets, interest financing on any additional or refinanced debt, and other appropriate adjustments that can be factually supported. See also Instruction 4 above.

6. When consummation of more than one transaction has occurred or is probable during a fiscal year, the pro forma financial information may be presented on a combined basis; however, in some circumstances (e.g., depending upon the combination of probable and consummated transactions, and the nature of the filing) it may be more useful to present the pro forma financial information on a disaggregated basis even though some or all of the transactions would not meet the tests of significance individually. For combined presentations, a note should explain the various transactions and disclose the maximum variances in the pro forma financial information which would occur for any of the possible combinations. If the pro forma financial information is presented in a proxy or information statement for purposes of obtaining shareholder approval of one of the transactions, the effects of that transaction must be clearly set forth.

7. Tax effects, if any, of pro forma adjustments normally should be calculated at the statutory rate in effect during the periods for which pro forma condensed income statements are presented and should be reflected as a separate pro forma adjustment.

(c) Periods to be presented. (1) A pro forma condensed balance sheet as of the end of the most recent period for which a consolidated balance sheet of the registrant is required by §210.3-01 shall be filed unless the transaction is already reflected in such balance sheet.

(2)(i) Pro forma condensed statements of income shall be filed for only the most recent fiscal year and for the period from the most recent fiscal year end to the most recent interim date for which a balance sheet is required. A pro forma condensed statement of income may be filed for the corresponding interim period of the preceding fiscal year. A pro forma condensed statement of income shall not be filed when the historical income statement reflects the transaction for the entire period.

(ii) For a business combination accounted for as a pooling of interests, the pro forma income statements (which are in effect a restatement of the historical income statements as if the combination had been consummated) shall be filed for all periods for which historical income statements of the registrant are required.

(3) Pro forma condensed statements of income shall be presented using the registrant's fiscal year end. If the most recent fiscal year end of any other entity involved in the transaction differs from the registrant's most recent fiscal year end by more than 93 days, the other entity's income statement shall be brought up to within 93 days of the registrant's most recent fiscal year end, if practicable. This updating could be accomplished by adding subsequent interim period results to the most recent fiscal year-end information and deducting the comparable preceding year interim period results. Disclosure shall be made of the periods combined and of the sales or revenues and income for any periods which were excluded from or included more than once in the condensed pro forma income statements (e.g., an interim period that is included both as part of the fiscal year and the subsequent interim period). For investment companies subject to §§210.6-01 to 210.6-10, the periods covered by the pro forma statements must be the same.

(4) Whenever unusual events enter into the determination of the results shown for the most recently completed fiscal year, the effect of such unusual events should be disclosed and consideration should be given to presenting a pro forma condensed income statement for the most recent twelve-month period in addition to those required in paragraph (c)(2)(i) above if the most recent twelve-month period is more representative of normal operations.

[47 FR 29837, July 9, 1982, as amended at 50 FR 49533, Dec. 3, 1985; 74 FR 18616, Apr. 23, 2009]

§210.11-03 Presentation of financial forecast.
(a) A financial forecast may be filed in lieu of the pro forma condensed statements of income required by §210.11-02(b)(1).

(1) The financial forecast shall cover a period of at least 12 months from the latest of (i) the most recent balance sheet included in the filing or (ii) the consummation date or estimated consummation date of the transaction.

(2) The forecasted statement of income shall be presented in the same degree of detail as the pro forma condensed statement of income required by §210.11-02(b)(3).

(3) Assumptions particularly relevant to the transaction and effects thereof should be clearly set forth.

(4) Historical condensed financial information of the registrant and the business acquired or to be acquired, if any, shall be presented for at least a recent 12 month period in parallel columns with the financial forecast.

(b) Such financial forecast shall be presented in accordance with the guidelines established by the American Institute of Certified Public Accountants.

(c) Forecasted earnings per share data shall be substituted for pro forma per share data.

(d) This rule does not permit the filing of a financial forecast in lieu of pro forma information required by generally accepted accounting principles.

Form and Content of Schedules

General

§210.12-01   Application of §§210.12-01 to 210.12-29.
These sections prescribe the form and content of the schedules required by §§210.5-04, 210.6-10, 210.6A-05, and 210.7-05.

[59 FR 65637, Dec. 20, 1994]

§§210.12-02--210.12-03   [Reserved]

§210.12-04   Condensed financial information of registrant.
(a) Provide condensed financial information as to financial position, cash flows and results of operations of the registrant as of the same dates and for the same periods for which audited consolidated financial statements are required. The financial information required need not be presented in greater detail than is required for condensed statements by §210.10-01(a) (2), (3) and (4). Detailed footnote disclosure which would normally be included with complete financial statements may be omitted with the exception of disclosures regarding material contingencies, long-term obligations and guarantees. Descriptions of significant provisions of the registrant's long-term obligations, mandatory dividend or redemption requirements of redeemable stocks, and guarantees of the registrant shall be provided along with a five-year schedule of maturities of debt. If the material contingencies, long-term obligations, redeemable stock requirements and guarantees of the registrant have been separately disclosed in the consolidated statements, they need not be repeated in this schedule.

(b) Disclose separately the amounts of cash dividends paid to the registrant for each of the last three fiscal years by consolidated subsidiaries, unconsolidated subsidiaries and 50 percent or less owned persons accounted for by the equity method, respectively.

[46 FR 56180, Nov. 16, 1981, as amended at 57 FR 45293, Oct. 1, 1992]

§210.12-05--210.12-08   [Reserved]

§210.12-09   Valuation and qualifying accounts.

Column A—Description[1]	Column B—Balance at beginning of period	Column C—Additions		Column D—Deductions—describe	Column E—Balance at end of period
		(1)—Charged to costs and expenses	(2)—Charged to other accounts—describe		

[1] List, by major classes, all valuation and qualifying accounts and reserves not included in specific schedules. Identify each class of valuation and qualifying accounts and reserves by descriptive title. Group (a) those valuation and qualifying accounts which are deducted in the balance sheet from the assets to which they apply and (b) those reserves which support the balance sheet caption, Reserves. Valuation and qualifying accounts and reserves as to which the additions, deductions, and balances were not individually significant may be grouped in one total and in such case the information called for under columns C and D need not be given.

[37 FR 14602, July 21, 1972. Redesignated and amended at 45 FR 63679, Sept. 25, 1980]

§§210.12-10--210.12-11   [Reserved]

For Management Investment Companies

§210.12-12   Investments in securities of unaffiliated issuers.
[For management investment companies only]

Col. A	Col. B	Col. C
Name of issuer and title of issue[1234]	Balance held at close of period. Number of shares—principal amount of bonds and notes[7]	Value of each item at close of period.[568910]

[1] Each issue shall be listed separately: Provided, however, that an amount not exceeding five percent of the total of Column C may be listed in one amount as "Miscellaneous securities," provided the securities so listed are not restricted, have been held for not more than one year prior to the date of the related balance sheet, and have not previously been reported by name to the shareholders of the person for which the schedule is filed or to any exchange, or set forth in any registration statement, application, or annual report or otherwise made available to the public. If any securities are listed as "Miscellaneous securities," briefly explain in a footnote what the term represents.

[2] Categorize the schedule by (i) the type of investment (such as common stocks, preferred stocks, convertible securities, fixed income securities, government securities, options purchased,

warrants, loan participations and assignments, commercial paper, bankers' acceptances, certificates of deposit, short-term securities, repurchase agreements, other investment companies, and so forth); and (ii) the related industry, country, or geographic region of the investment. Short-term debt instruments (i.e., debt instruments whose maturities or expiration dates at the time of acquisition are one year or less) of the same issuer may be aggregated, in which case the range of interest rates and maturity dates shall be indicated. For issuers of periodic payment plan certificates and unit investment trusts, list separately: (i) Trust shares in trusts created or serviced by the depositor or sponsor of this trust; (ii) trust shares in other trusts; and (iii) securities of other investment companies. Restricted securities shall not be combined with unrestricted securities of the same issuer. Repurchase agreements shall be stated separately showing for each the name of the party or parties to the agreement, the date of the agreement, the total amount to be received upon repurchase, the repurchase date and description of securities subject to the repurchase agreements.

[3] For options purchased, all information required by §210.12-13 for options contracts written should be shown. Options on underlying investments where the underlying investment would otherwise be presented in accordance with §§210.12-12, 12-13A, 12-13B, 12-13C, or 12-13D should include the description of the underlying investment as would be required by §§210.12-12, 12-13A, 12-13B, 12-13C, or 12-13D as part of the description of the option.

[4] Indicate the interest rate or preferential dividend rate and maturity date, as applicable, for preferred stocks, convertible securities, fixed income securities, government securities, loan participations and assignments, commercial paper, bankers' acceptances, certificates of deposit, short-term securities, repurchase agreements, or other instruments with a stated rate of income. For variable rate securities, indicate a description of the reference rate and spread and: (1) The end of period interest rate or (2) disclose the end of period reference rate for each reference rate described in the Schedule in a note to the Schedule. For securities with payment in kind income, disclose the rate paid in kind.

[5] The subtotals for each category of investments, subdivided both by type of investment and industry, country or geographic region, shall be shown together with their percentage value compared to net assets. (§§210.6-04.19 or 210.6-05.4.)

[6] Column C shall be totaled. The total of Column C shall agree with the correlative amounts shown on the related balance sheet.

[7] Indicate by an appropriate symbol each issue of securities which is non-income producing. Evidences of indebtedness and preferred shares may be deemed to be income producing if, on the respective last interest payment date or date for the declaration of dividends prior to the date of the related balance sheet, there was only a partial payment of interest or a declaration of only a partial amount of the dividends payable; in such case, however, each such issue shall be indicated by an appropriate symbol referring to a note to the effect that, on the last interest or dividend date, only partial interest was paid or partial dividends declared. If, on such respective last interest or dividend date, no interest was paid or no cash or in kind dividends declared, the issue shall not be deemed to be income producing. Common shares shall not be

deemed to be income producing unless, during the last year preceding the date of the related balance sheet, there was at least one dividend paid upon such common shares.

[8] Indicate by an appropriate symbol each issue of restricted securities. State the following in a footnote: (a) As to each such issue: (1) Acquisition date, (2) carrying value per unit of investment at date of related balance sheet, e.g., a percentage of current market value of unrestricted securities of the same issuer, etc., and (3) the cost of such securities; (b) as to each issue acquired during the year preceding the date of the related balance sheet, the carrying value per unit of investment of unrestricted securities of the same issuer at: (1) The day the purchase price was agreed to; and (2) the day on which an enforceable right to acquire such securities was obtained; and (c) the aggregate value of all restricted securities and the percentage which the aggregate value bears to net assets.

[9] Indicate by an appropriate symbol each issue of securities whose value was determined using significant unobservable inputs.

[10] Indicate by an appropriate symbol each issue of securities held in connection with open put or call option contracts, loans for short sales, or where any portion of the issue is on loan.

[81 FR 82014, Nov. 18, 2016]

§210.12-12A   Investments—securities sold short.
[For management investment companies only]

Col. A	Col. B	Col. C
Name of issuer and title of issue[123]	Balance of short position at close of period (number of shares)	Value of each open short position[456]

[1] Each issue shall be listed separately.

[2] Categorize the schedule as required by instruction 2 of §210.12-12.

[3] Indicate the interest rate or preferential dividend rate and maturity date, as applicable, for preferred stocks, convertible securities, fixed income securities, government securities, loan participations and assignments, commercial paper, bankers' acceptances, certificates of deposit, short-term securities, repurchase agreements, or other instruments with a stated rate of income. For variable rate securities, indicate a description of the reference rate and spread and: (1) The end of period interest rate or (2) disclose the end of period reference rate for each reference rate described in the Schedule in a note to the Schedule. For securities with payment in kind income, disclose the rate paid in kind.

[4] The subtotals for each category of investments, subdivided both by type of investment and industry, country, or geographic region, shall be shown together with their percentage value compared to net assets.

[5] Column C shall be totaled. The total of Column C shall agree with the correlative amounts shown on the related balance sheet.

[6] Indicate by an appropriate symbol each issue of securities whose value was determined using significant unobservable inputs.

[81 FR 82015, Nov. 18, 2016]

§210.12-12B Summary schedule of investments in securities of unaffiliated issuers.

Column A	Column B	Column C	Column D
Name of issuer and title of issue[1345678]	Balance held at close of period. Number of shares—principal amount of bonds and notes [10]	Value of each item at close of period[29111213]	Percentage value compared to net assets.

[1] Categorize the schedule by (a) the type of investment (such as common stocks, preferred stocks, convertible securities, fixed income securities, government securities, options purchased, warrants, loan participations and assignments, commercial paper, bankers' acceptances, certificates of deposit, short-term securities, repurchase agreements, other investment companies, and so forth); and (b) the related industry, country or geographic region of the investment.

[2] The subtotals for each category of investments, subdivided both by type of investment and industry, country, or geographic region, shall be shown together with their percentage value compared to net assets.

[3] Indicate the interest rate or preferential dividend rate and maturity date, as applicable, for preferred stocks, convertible securities, fixed income securities, government securities, loan participations and assignments, commercial paper, bankers' acceptances, certificates of deposit, short-term securities, repurchase agreements, or other instruments with a stated rate of income. For variable rate securities, indicate a description of the reference rate and spread and: (1) The end of period interest rate or (2) disclose the end of period reference rate for each reference rate described in the Schedule in a note to the Schedule. For securities with payment in kind income, disclose the rate paid in kind.

[4] Except as provided in note 6, list separately the 50 largest issues and any other issue the value of which exceeded one percent of net asset value of the registrant as of the close of the period. For purposes of the list (including, in the case of short-term debt instruments, the first sentence of note 4), aggregate and treat as a single issue, respectively, (a) short-term debt instruments (i.e., debt instruments whose maturities or expiration dates at the time of acquisition are one year or less) of the same issuer (indicating the range of interest rates and maturity dates); and (b) fully collateralized repurchase agreements (indicate in a footnote the range of dates of the repurchase agreements, the total purchase price of the securities, the total amount to be received upon repurchase, the range of repurchase dates, and description of securities subject to the repurchase agreements). Restricted and unrestricted securities of the same issue should be aggregated for purposes of determining whether the issue is among the 50 largest issues, but should not be combined in the schedule. For purposes of determining whether the value of an issue exceeds one percent of net asset value, aggregate and treat as a single issue all securities of any one issuer, except that all fully collateralized repurchase agreements shall be aggregated and treated as a single issue. The U.S. Treasury and each agency, instrumentality, or corporation,

144

including each government-sponsored entity, that issues U.S. government securities is a separate issuer.

[5] For options purchased, all information required by §210.12-13 for options contracts written should be shown. Options on underlying investments where the underlying investment would otherwise be presented in accordance with §§210.12-12, 12-13A, 12-13B, 12-13C, or 12-13D should include the description of the underlying investment as would be required by §§210.12-12, 12-13A, 12-13B, 12-13C, or 12-13D as part of the description of the option.

[6] If multiple securities of an issuer aggregate to greater than one percent of net asset value, list each issue of the issuer separately (including separate listing of restricted and unrestricted securities of the same issue) except that the following may be aggregated and listed as a single issue: (a) Fixed-income securities of the same issuer which are not among the 50 largest issues and whose value does not exceed one percent of net asset value of the registrant as of the close of the period (indicating the range of interest rates and maturity dates); and (b) U.S. government securities of a single agency, instrumentality, or corporation, which are not among the 50 largest issues and whose value does not exceed one percent of net asset value of the registrant as of the close of the period (indicating the range of interest rates and maturity dates). For each category identified pursuant to note 1, group all issues that are neither separately listed nor included in a group of securities that is listed in the aggregate as a single issue in a sub-category labeled "Other securities," and provide the information for Columns C and D.

[7] Any securities that would be required to be listed separately or included in a group of securities that is listed in the aggregate as a single issue may be listed in one amount as "Miscellaneous securities," provided the securities so listed are eligible to be, and are, categorized as "Miscellaneous securities" in the registrant's Schedule of Investments in Securities of Unaffiliated Issuers required under §210.12-12. However, if any security that is included in "Miscellaneous securities" would otherwise be required to be included in a group of securities that is listed in the aggregate as a single issue, the remaining securities of that group must nonetheless be listed as required by notes 4 and 5 even if the remaining securities alone would not otherwise be required to be listed in this manner (e.g., because the combined value of the security listed in "Miscellaneous securities" and the remaining securities of the same issuer exceeds one percent of net asset value, but the value of the remaining securities alone does not exceed one percent of net asset value).

[8] If any securities are listed as "Miscellaneous securities" pursuant to note 6 or "Other securities" pursuant to note 5, briefly explain in a footnote what those terms represent.

[9] Total Column C. The total of Column C should equal the total shown on the related balance sheet for investments in securities of unaffiliated issuers.

[10] Indicate by an appropriate symbol each issue of securities which is non-income producing. Evidences of indebtedness and preferred shares may be deemed to be income producing if, on the respective last interest payment date or date for the declaration of dividends prior to the date of the related balance sheet, there was only a partial payment of interest or a declaration of only a partial amount of the dividends payable; in such case, however, each such

issue shall be indicated by an appropriate symbol referring to a note to the effect that, on the last interest or dividend date, only partial interest was paid or partial dividends declared. If, on such respective last interest or dividend date, no interest was paid or no cash or in kind dividends declared, the issue shall not be deemed to be income producing. Common shares shall not be deemed to be income producing unless, during the last year preceding the date of the related balance sheet, there was at least one dividend paid upon such common shares.

[11] Indicate by an appropriate symbol each issue of restricted securities. State the following in a footnote: (a) As to each such issue: (1) Acquisition date, (2) carrying value per unit of investment at date of related balance sheet, e.g., a percentage of current market value of unrestricted securities of the same issuer, etc., and (3) the cost of such securities; (b) as to each issue acquired during the year preceding the date of the related balance sheet, the carrying value per unit of investment of unrestricted securities of the same issuer at: (1) The day the purchase price was agreed to; and (2) the day on which an enforceable right to acquire such securities was obtained; and (c) the aggregate value of all restricted securities and the percentage which the aggregate value bears to net assets.

[12] Indicate by an appropriate symbol each issue of securities whose value was determined using significant unobservable inputs.

[13] Indicate by an appropriate symbol each issue of securities held in connection with open put or call option contracts, loans for short sales, or where any portion of the issue is on loan.

[81 FR 82015, Nov. 18, 2016]

§210.12-12C   [Reserved]

§210.12-13   Open option contracts written.
[For management investment companies only]

Col. A	Col. B	Col. C	Col. D	Col. E	Col. F	Col. G
Description[1 2 3]	Counterparty[4]	Number of contracts[5]	Notional amount	Exercise price	Expiration date	Value.[6 7 8]

[1] Information as to put options shall be shown separately from information as to call options.

[2] Options where descriptions, counterparties, exercise prices or expiration dates differ shall be listed separately.

[3] Options on underlying investments where the underlying investment would otherwise be presented in accordance with §§210.12-12, 12-13A, 12-13B, 12-13C, or 12-13D should include the description of the underlying investment as would be required by §§210.12-12, 12-13A, 12-13B, 12-13C, or 12-13D as part of the description of the option.

If the underlying investment is an index or basket of investments, and the components are publicly available on a Web site as of the balance sheet date, identify the index or basket. If the underlying investment is an index or basket of investments, the components are not publicly available on a Web site as of the balance sheet date, and the notional amount of the option contract does not exceed one percent of the net asset value of the registrant as of the close of the period, identify the index or basket. If the underlying investment is an index or basket of investments, the components are not publicly available on a Web site as of the balance sheet date, and the notional amount of the option contract exceeds one percent of the net asset value of the registrant as of the close of the period, provide a description of the index or custom basket and list separately: (i) The 50 largest components in the index or custom basket and (ii) any other components where the notional value for that components exceeds 1% of the notional value of the index or custom basket. For each investment separately listed, include the description of the underlying investment as would be required by §§210.12-12, 12-13, 12-13A, 12-13B, or 12-13D as part of the description, the quantity held (e.g. the number of shares for common stocks, principal amount for fixed income securities), the value at the close of the period, and the percentage value when compared to the custom basket's net assets.

[4] Not required for exchange traded or centrally cleared options.

[5] If the number of shares subject to option is substituted for number of contracts, the column name shall reflect that change.

[6] Indicate by an appropriate symbol each investment which cannot be sold because of restrictions or conditions applicable to the investment.

[7] Indicate by an appropriate symbol each investment whose value was determined using significant unobservable inputs.

[8] Column G shall be totaled and shall agree with the correlative amount shown on the related balance sheet.

[81 FR 82016, Nov. 18, 2016]

§210.12-13A   Open futures contracts.
[For management investment companies only]

Col. A	Col. B	Col. C	Col. D	Col. E	Col. F
Description[1 2 3 4 5]	Number of contracts	Expiration date	Notional amount[6]	Value	Unrealized appreciation/depreciation.

[1] Information as to long purchases of futures contracts shall be shown separately from information as to futures contracts sold short.

[2] Futures contracts where descriptions or expiration dates differ shall be listed separately.

[3] Description should include the name of the reference asset or index.

147

Indicate by an appropriate symbol each investment which cannot be sold because of restrictions or conditions applicable to the investment.

[5] Indicate by an appropriate symbol each investment whose value was determined using significant unobservable inputs.

[6] Notional amount shall be the current notional amount at close of period.

[81 FR 82017, Nov. 18, 2016]

§210.12-13B Open forward foreign currency contracts.
[For management investment companies only]

Col. A	Col. B	Col. C	Col. D	Col. E
Amount and description of currency to be purchased[1]	Amount and description of currency to be sold[1]	Counterparty	Settlement date	Unrealized appreciation/ depreciation.[2][3][4]

[1] Forward foreign currency contracts where description of currency purchased, description of currency sold, counterparty, or settlement dates differ shall be listed separately.

[2] Indicate by an appropriate symbol each investment which cannot be sold because of restrictions or conditions applicable to the investment.

[3] Indicate by an appropriate symbol each investment whose value was determined using significant unobservable inputs.

[4] Column E shall be totaled and shall agree with the total of correlative amount(s) shown on the related balance sheet.

[81 FR 82017, Nov. 18, 2016]

§210.12-13C Open swap contracts.
[For management investment companies only]

Col. A	Col. B	Col. C	Col. D	Col. E	Col. F	Col. G	Col. H
Description and terms of payments to be received from another party[1][2][3]	Description and terms of payments to be paid to another party[1][2][3]	Counterparty[4]	Maturity date	Notional amount	Value	Upfront payments/receipts	Unrealized appreciation/ depreciation.[5][6][7]

[1] List each major category of swaps by descriptive title (e.g., credit default swaps, interest rate swaps, total return swaps). Credit default swaps where protection is sold shall be listed separately from credit default swaps where protection is purchased.

[2] Swaps where description, counterparty, or maturity dates differ shall be listed separately within each major category.

[3] Description should include information sufficient for a user of financial information to understand the terms of payments to be received and paid. (e.g. For a credit default swap, including, among other things, description of reference obligation(s) or index, financing rate to be paid or received, and payment frequency. For an interest rate swap, this may include, among other things, whether floating rate is paid or received, fixed interest rate, floating interest rate, and payment frequency. For a total return swap, this may include, among other things, description of reference asset(s) or index, financing rate, and payment frequency.) If the reference instrument is an index or basket of investments, and the components are publicly available on a Web site as of the balance sheet date, identify the index or basket.If the reference instrument is an index or basket of investments, the components are not publicly available on a Web site as of the balance sheet date, and the notional amount of the swap contract does not exceed one percent of the net asset value of the registrant as of the close of the period, identify the index or basket. If the reference instrument is an index or basket of investments, the components are not publicly available on a Web site as of the balance sheet date, and the notional amount of the swap contract exceeds one percent of the net asset value of the registrant as of the close of the period provide a description of the index or custom basket and list separately: (i) The 50 largest components in the index or custom basket and (ii) any other components where the notional value for that components exceeds 1% of the notional value of the index or custom basket. For each investment separately listed, include the description of the underlying investment as would be required by §§210.12-12, 210.12-13, 210.12-13A, 210.12-13B, or 210.12-13D as part of the description, the quantity held (e.g., the number of shares for common stocks, principal amount for fixed income securities), the value at the close of the period, and the percentage value when compared to the custom basket's net assets.

[4] Not required for exchange-traded or centrally cleared swaps.

[5] Indicate by an appropriate symbol each investment which cannot be sold because of restrictions or conditions applicable to the investment.

[6] Indicate by an appropriate symbol each investment whose value was determined using significant unobservable inputs.

[7] Columns G and H shall be totaled and shall agree with the total of correlative amount(s) shown on the related balance sheet.

[81 FR 82017, Nov. 18, 2016]

§210.12-13D   Investments other than those presented in §§210.12-12, 12-12A, 12-12B, 12-13, 12-13A, 12-13B, and 12-13C.
[For management investment companies only]

Col. A	Col. B	Col. C
Description[1][2][3]	Balance held at close of period—quantity[4][5]	Value of each item at close of period.[6][7][8][9]

[1] Each investment where any portion of the description differs shall be listed separately.

[2] Categorize the schedule by (i) the type of investment (such as real estate, commodities, and so forth); and, as applicable, (ii) the related industry, country, or geographic region of the investment.

[3] Description should include information sufficient for a user of financial information to understand the nature and terms of the investment, which may include, among other things, reference security, asset or index, currency, geographic location, payment terms, payment rates, call or put feature, exercise price, expiration date, and counterparty for non-exchange-traded investments.

[4] If practicable, indicate the quantity or measure in appropriate units.

[5] Indicate by an appropriate symbol each investment which is non-income producing.

[6] Indicate by an appropriate symbol each investment which cannot be sold because of restrictions or conditions applicable to the investment.

[7] Indicate by an appropriate symbol each investment whose value was determined using significant unobservable inputs.

[8] Indicate by an appropriate symbol investment subject to option. State in a footnote: (a) The quantity subject to option, (b) nature of option contract, (c) option price, and (d) dates within which options may be exercised.

[9] Column C shall be totaled and shall agree with the correlative amount shown on the related balance sheet.

[81 FR 82018, Nov. 18, 2016]

§210.12-14 Investments in and advances to affiliates.
[For management investment companies only]

Col. A	Col. B	Col. C	Col. D	Col. E	Col. F
Name of issuer and title of issue or nature of indebtedness[1][2][3]	Number of shares—principal amount of bonds, notes and other indebtedness held at close of period	Net realized gain or loss for the period[4][6]	Net increase or decrease in unrealized appreciation or depreciation for the period[4][6]	Amount of dividends or interest[4][6] (1) Credited to income (2) Other	Value of each item at close of period.[4][5][7][8][9]

1 (a) List each issue separately and group (1) Investments in majority-owned subsidiaries; (2) other controlled companies; and (3) other affiliates. (b) If during the period there has been any increase or decrease in the amount of investment in and advance to any affiliate, state in a footnote (or if there have been changes to numerous affiliates, in a supplementary schedule) (1) name of each issuer and title of issue or nature of indebtedness; (2) balance at beginning of period; (3) gross additions; (4) gross reductions; (5) balance at close of period as shown in Column E. Include in the footnote or schedule comparable information as to affiliates in which there was an investment at any time during the period even though there was no investment at the close of the period of report.

2 Categorize the schedule as required by instruction 2 of §210.12-12.

3 Indicate the interest rate or preferential dividend rate and maturity date, as applicable, for preferred stocks, convertible securities, fixed income securities, government securities, loan participations and assignments, commercial paper, bankers' acceptances, certificates of deposit, short-term securities, repurchase agreements, or other instruments with a stated rate of income. For variable rate securities, indicate a description of the reference rate and spread and: (1) The end of period interest rate or (2) disclose the end of period reference rate for each reference rate described in the Schedule in a note to the Schedule. For securities with payment in kind income, disclose the rate paid in kind.

4 Columns C, D, E, and F shall be totaled. The totals of Column F shall agree with the correlative amount shown on the related balance sheet.

5 (a) Indicate by an appropriate symbol each issue of restricted securities. The information required by instruction 8 of §210.12-12 shall be given in a footnote. (b) Indicate by an appropriate symbol each issue of securities subject to option. The information required by §210.12-13 shall be given in a footnote.

6 (a) Include in Column E (1) as to each issue held at the close of the period, the dividends or interest included in caption 1 of the statement of operations. In addition, show as the final item in Column E (1) the aggregate of dividends and interest included in the statement of operations in respect of investments in affiliates not held at the close of the period. The total of this column shall agree with the correlative amount shown on the related statement of operations.

(b) Include in Column E (2) all other dividends and interest. Explain in an appropriate footnote the treatment accorded each item.

(c) Indicate by an appropriate symbol all non-cash dividends and interest and explain the circumstances in a footnote.

(d) Indicate by an appropriate symbol each issue of securities which is non-income producing. Evidences of indebtedness and preferred shares may be deemed to be income producing if, on the respective last interest payment date or date for the declaration of dividends prior to the date of the related balance sheet, there was only a partial payment of interest or a declaration of only a partial amount of the dividends payable; in such case, however, each such issue shall be indicated by an appropriate symbol referring to a note to the effect that, on the last interest or dividend date, only partial interest was paid or partial dividends declared. If, on such respective last interest or dividend date, no interest was paid or no cash or in kind dividends declared, the issue shall not be deemed to be income producing. Common shares shall not be deemed to be income producing unless, during the last year preceding the date of the related balance sheet, there was at least one dividend paid upon such common shares.

(e) Include in Column C (1) as to each issue held at the close of the period, the realized gain or loss included in §210.6-07.7 of the statement of operations. In addition, show as the final item in Column C (1) the aggregate of realized gain or loss included in the statement of operations in respect of investments in affiliates not held at the close of the period. The total of this column shall agree with the correlative amount shown on the related statement of operations.

(f) Include in Column D (1) as to each issue held at the close of the period, the net increase or decrease in unrealized appreciation or depreciation included in §210.6-07 .7 of the statement of operations. In addition, show as the final item in Column D (1) the aggregate of increase or decrease in unrealized appreciation or depreciation included in the statement of operations in respect of investments in affiliates not held at the close of the period. The total of this column shall agree with the correlative amount shown on the related statement of operations.

[7] The subtotals for each category of investments, subdivided both by type of investment and industry, country, or geographic region, shall be shown together with their percentage value compared to net assets.

[8] Indicate by an appropriate symbol each issue of securities whose value was determined using significant unobservable inputs.

[9] Indicate by an appropriate symbol each issue of securities held in connection with open put or call option contracts, loans for short sales, or where any portion of the issue is on loan.

[81 FR 82018, Nov. 18, 2016]

§210.12-15 Summary of investments—other than investments in related parties.
[For Insurance Companies]

Column A	Column B	Column C	Column D
Type of investment	Cost[1]	Value	Amount at which shown in the balance sheet[2]
Fixed maturities:			
Bonds:			
United States Government and government agencies and authorities			
States, municipalities and political subdivisions			
Foreign governments			
Public utilities			
Convertibles and bonds with warrants attached[3]			
All other corporate bonds			
Certificates of deposit			
Redeemable preferred stock			
Total fixed maturities			
Equity securities:			
Common stocks:			
Public utilities			
Banks, trust and insurance companies			
Industrial, miscellaneous and all other			
Nonredeemable preferred stocks			
Total equity securities			
Mortgage loans on real estate			
Real estate[4]			
Policy loans			
Other long-term investments			
Short-term investments			
Total investments			

[1] Original cost of equity securities and, as to fixed maturities, original cost reduced by repayments and adjusted for amortization of premiums or accrual of discounts.

[2] If the amount at which shown in the balance sheet is different from the amount shown in either column B or C, state the reason for such difference. The total of this column should agree with the balance sheet.

[3] All convertibles and bonds with warrants shall be included in this caption, regardless of issuer.

[4] State separately any real estate acquired in satisfaction of debt.

[46 FR 54337, Nov. 2, 1981]

§210.12-16 Supplementary insurance information.
[For insurance companies]

Column A	Column B	Column C	Column D	Column E	Column F	Column G	Column H	Column I	Column J	Column K
Segment[1]	Deferred policy acquisition cost (caption 7)	Future policy benefits, losses, claims and loss expenses (caption 13-a-1)	Unearned premiums (caption 13-a-2)	Other policy claims and benefits payable (caption 13-a-3)	Premium revenue (caption 1)	Net investment income (caption 2)[3]	Benefits, claims, losses, and settlement expenses (caption 5)	Amortization of deferred policy acquisition costs[4]	Other operating expenses[3][4]	Premiums written[2]
Total[5]										

[1] Segments shown should be the same as those presented in the footnote disclosures called for by generally accepted accounting principles.

[2] Does not apply to life insurance or title insurance. This amount should include premiums from reinsurance assumed, and be net of premiums on reinsurance ceded.

[3] State the basis for allocation of net investment income and, where applicable, other operating expenses.

[4] The total of columns I and J should agree with the amount shown for income statement caption 7.

[5] Totals should agree with the indicated balance sheet and income statement caption amounts, where a caption number is shown.

[46 FR 54338, Nov. 2, 1981, as amended at 57 FR 45293, Oct. 1, 1992; 64 FR 1734, Jan. 12, 1999]

§210.12-17 Reinsurance.
[For insurance companies]

Column A	Column B	Column C	Column D	Column E	Column F
	Gross amount	Ceded to other companies[1]	Assumed from other companies	Net amount[2]	Percentage of amount assumed to net[3]
Life insurance in force					
Premiums:					
Life insurance					
Accident and health insurance					
Property and liability insurance					
Title insurance					
Total premiums					

[1] Indicate in a note any amounts of reinsurance or coinsurance income netted against premiums ceded.

[2] This Column represents the total of column B less column C plus column D. The total premiums in this column should represent the amount of premium revenue on the income statement.

[3] Calculated as the amount in column D divided by amount in column E.

[46 FR 54338, Nov. 2, 1981]

§210.12-18 Supplemental information (for property-casualty insurance underwriters).

Affiliation with registrant	Deferred policy acquisition costs	Reserves for unpaid claims and claim adjustment expenses	Discount, if any, deducted in column c[4]	Unearned premiums	Earned premiums	Net investment income	Claims and claim adjustment expenses incurred related to		Amortization of deferred policy acquisition costs	Paid claims and claim adjustment expenses	Premiums written
							(1) Current year	(2) Prior years			
Column A	Column B	Column C	Column D	Column E	Column F	Column G	Column H		Column I	Column J	Column K
(a) Consolidated property-casualty entities[2]											
(b) Unconsolidated property-casualty subsidiaries[2][3]											
(c) Proportionate share of registrant and its subsidiaries' 50%-or-less-owned property-casualty equity investees[2][3]											

[1] Information included in audited financial statements, including other schedules, need not be repeated in this schedule. Columns B, C, D, and E are as of the balance sheet dates, columns F, G, H, I, J, and K are for the same periods for which income statements are presented in the registrant's audited consolidated financial statements.

[2] Present combined or consolidated amounts, as appropriate for each category, after intercompany eliminations.

[3] Information is not required here for 50%-or-less-owned equity investees that file similar information with the Commission as registrants in their own right, if that fact and the name of the affiliated registrant is stated. If ending reserves in any category (a), (b), or (c) above is less than 5% of the total reserves otherwise required to be reported in this schedule, that category may be omitted and that fact so noted. If the amount of the reserves attributable to 50%-or-less-owned equity investors that file this information as registrants in their own right exceeds 95% of the total category (c) reserves, information for the other 50%-or-less-owned equity investees need not be provided.

[4] Disclose in a footnote to this schedule the rate, or range of rates, estimated if necessary, at which the discount was computed for each category.

[49 FR 47599, Dec. 6, 1984]

For face-amount certificate investment companies

Source: Sections 210.12-21 to 210.12-41 appear at 16 FR 348, Jan. 13, 1951, unless otherwise noted. Redesignated at 45 FR 63679, Sept. 25, 1980.

§210.12-21 Investments in securities of unaffiliated issuers.

Column A—Name of issuer and title of issue[1]	Column B—Balance held at close of period. Number of shares—principal amount of bonds and notes[2]	Column C—Cost of each item[3] [4]	Column D—Value of each item at close of period[3] [5]

[1] (a) The required information is to be given as to all securities held as of the close of the period of report. Each issue shall be listed separately.

(b) Indicate by an appropriate symbol those securities which are non-income-producing securities. Evidences of indebtedness and preferred shares may be deemed to be income-producing if, on the respective last interest payment date or dates for the declaration of dividends prior to the date of the related balance sheet, there was only a partial payment of interest or a declaration of only a partial amount of the dividends payable; in such case, however, each such issue shall be indicated by an appropriate symbol referring to a note to the effect that, on the last interest or dividend date, only partial interest was paid or partial dividends declared. If, on such respective last interest or dividend date, no interest was paid or no dividends declared, the issue shall not be deemed to be income-producing. Common shares shall not be deemed to be income-producing unless, during the last year preceding the date of the related balance sheet, there was at least one dividend paid upon such common shares. List separately (1) bonds; (2) preferred shares; (3) common shares. Within each of these subdivisions classify according to type of business, insofar as practicable: e.g., investment companies, railroads, utilities, banks, insurance companies, or industrials. Give totals for each group, subdivision, and class.

[2] Indicate any securities subject to option at the end of the most recent period and state in a note the amount subject to option, the option prices, and the dates within which such options may be exercised.

[3] Columns C and D shall be totaled. The totals of columns C and D should agree with the correlative amounts required to be shown by the related balance sheet captions. State in a footnote to column C the aggregate cost for Federal income tax purposes.

156

^{4} If any investments have been written down or reserved against by such companies pursuant to §210.6-21(f), indicate each such item by means of an appropriate symbol and explain in a footnote.

^{5} Where value is determined on any other basis than closing prices reported on any national securities exchange, explain such other basis in a footnote.

[47 FR 56844, Dec. 21, 1982]

§210.12-22 Investments in and advances to affiliates and income thereon.

Column A—Name of issuer and title of issue or amount of indebtedness^1	Column B—Balance held at close of period—Number of shares—principal amount of bonds, notes and other indebtedness^2	Column C—Cost of each item^3 ^{4}	Column D—Amount at which carried at close of period^4 ^{5}	Column E—Amount of dividends or interest^4 ^{6}		Column F—Amount of equity in net profit and loss for the period^7
				(1)—Credited to income	(2)—Other	

^{1} (a) The required information is to be given as to all investments in affiliates as of the close of the period. See captions 10, 13 and 20 of §210.6-22. List each issue and group separately (1) investments in majority-owned subsidiaries, segregating subsidiaries consolidated; (2) other controlled companies; and (3) other affiliates. Give totals for each group. If operations of any controlled companies are different in character from those of the registrant, group such affiliates within divisions (1) and (2) by type of activities.

(b) Changes during the period. If during the period there has been any increase or decrease in the amount of investment in any affiliate, state in a footnote (or if there have been changes as to numerous affiliates, in a supplementary schedule) (1) name of each issuer and title of issue; (2) balance at beginning of period; (3) gross purchases and additions; (4) gross sales and reductions; (5) balance at close of period as shown in column C. Include in such footnote or schedule comparable information as to affiliates in which there was an investment at any time during the period even though there was no investment in such affiliate as of the close of such period.

^{2} Indicate any securities subject to option at the end of the most recent period and state in a footnote the amount subject to option, the option prices, and the dates within which such options may be exercised.

^{3} If the cost in column C represents other than cash expenditure, explain.

^{4} (a) Columns C, D and E shall be totaled. The totals of columns C and D should agree with correlative amounts required to be shown by the related balance sheet captions. State in a footnote the aggregate cost for Federal income tax purposes.

157

(b) If any investments have been written down or reserved against by such companies pursuant to §210.6-21(f), indicate each such item by means of an appropriate symbol and explain in a footnote.

[5] State the basis of determining the amounts shown in column D.

[6] Show in column E(1) as to each issue held at close of period, the dividends or interest included in caption 1 of the profit and loss or income statement. In addition, show as the final item in column E(1) the aggregate dividends and interest included in the profit and loss or income statement in respect of investments in affiliates not held at the close of the period. The total of this column should agree with the amounts shown under such caption. Include in column E(2) all other dividends and interest. Explain briefly in an appropriate footnote the treatment accorded each item. Identify by an appropriate symbol all non-cash dividends and explain the circumstances in a footnote. See §§210.6-22(b) and 210.6-23(a).

[7] The information required by column F need be furnished only as to controlled companies. The equity in the net profit and loss of each person required to be listed separately shall be computed on an individual basis. In addition, there may be submitted the information required as computed on the basis of the statements of each such person and its subsidiaries consolidated.

§210.12-23 Mortgage loans on real estate and interest earned on mortgages.[1]

Part 1—Mortgage loans on real estate at close of period						Part 2—Interest earned on mortgages	
Column A—List by classification indicated below[2][3][7]	Column B—Prior liens[2]	Column C—Carrying amount of mortgage[8][9][10][11]	Column D—Amount of principal unpaid at close of period		Column E—Amount of mortgage being foreclosed	Column F—Interest due and accrued at end of period[6]	Column G—Interest income earned applicable to period[5]
			(1)—Total	(2)—Subject to delinquent interest[4]			
Liens on:							
Farms (total)							
Residential (total)							
Apartments and business (total)							
Unimproved (total)							
Total[12]							

[1] All money columns shall be totaled.

[2] If mortgages represent other than first liens, list separately in a schedule in a like manner, indicating briefly the nature of the lien. Information need not be furnished as to such liens which are fully insured or wholly guaranteed by an agency of the United States Government.

[3] In a separate schedule classify by states in which the mortgaged property is located the total amounts in support of columns B, C, D and E.

[4] (a) Interest in arrears for less than 3 months may be disregarded in computing the total amount of principal subject to delinquent interest.

(b) Of the total principal amount, state the amount acquired from controlled and other affiliates.

[5] In order to reconcile the total of column G with the amount shown in the profit and loss or income statement, interest income earned applicable to period from mortgages sold or canceled during period should be added to the total of this column.

[6] If the information required by columns F and G is not reasonably available because the obtaining thereof would involve unreasonable effort or expense, such information may be omitted if the registrant shall include a statement showing that unreasonable effort or expense would be involved. In such an event, state in column G for each of the above classes of mortgage loans the average gross rate of interest on mortgage loans held at the end of the fiscal period.

[7] Each mortgage loan included in column C in an amount in excess of $500,000 shall be listed separately. Loans from $100,000 to $500,000 shall be grouped by $50,000 groups, indicating the number of loans in each group.

[8] In a footnote to this schedule, furnish a reconciliation, in the following form, of the carrying amount of mortgage loans at the beginning of the period with the total amount shown in column C:

Balance at beginning of period	$	
Additions during period:		
New mortgage loans	$	
Other (describe)		
Deductions during period:		
Collections of principal	$	
Foreclosures		
Cost of mortgages sold		
Amortization of premium		
Other (describe)		
Balance at close of period	$	

If additions represent other than cash expenditures, explain. If any of the changes during the period result from transactions, directly or indirectly with affiliates, explain the bases of such transactions, and amounts involved. State the aggregate amount of mortgages (a) renewed and (b) extended. If the carrying amount of the new mortgages is in excess of the unpaid amount (not including interest) of prior mortgages, explain.

[9] If any item of mortgage loans on real estate investments has been written down or reserved against pursuant to §210.6-21 describe the item and explain the basis for the write-down or reserve.

[10] State in a footnote to column C the aggregate cost for Federal income tax purposes.

159

[11] If the total amount shown in column C includes intercompany profits, state the bases of the transactions resulting in such profits and, if practicable, state the amounts thereof.

[12] Summarize the aggregate amounts for each column applicable to captions 6(b), 6(c) and 12 of §210.6-22.

[16 FR 348, Jan. 13, 1951, as amended at 16 FR 2655, Mar. 24, 1951]

§210.12-24 Real estate owned and rental income.[1]

Part 1—Real estate owned at end of period						Part 2—Rental income			
Column A—List classification of property as indicated below[2 3]	Column B—Amount of incombrances	Column C—Initial cost to company	Column D—Cost of improvements, etc.	Column E—Amount at which carried at close of period[4 5 6 7]	Column F—Reserve for depreciation	Column G—Rents due and accrued at end of period	Column H—Total rental income applicable to period	Column I—Expended for interest, taxes, repairs and expenses	Column J—Net income applicable to period
Farms									
Residential									
Apartments and business									
Unimproved									
Total[8]									
Rent from properties sold during period									
Total									

[1] All money columns shall be totaled.

[2] Each item of property included in column E in an amount in excess of $100,000 shall be listed separately.

[3] In a separate schedule classify by states in which the real estate owned is located the total amounts in support of columns E and F.

[4] In a footnote to this schedule, furnish a reconciliation, in the following form, of the total amount at which real estate was carried at the beginning of the period with the total amount shown in column E:

Balance at beginning of period		$
Additions during period:		
Acquisitions through foreclosure	$	
Other acquisitions		
Improvements, etc		
Other (describe)		
Deductions during period:		
Cost of real estate sold	$	
Other (describe)		
Balance at close of period		$

If additions, except acquisitions through foreclosure, represent other than cash expenditures, explain. If any of the changes during the period result from transactions, directly or indirectly, with affiliates, explain and state the amount of any intercompany gain or loss.

[5] If any item of real estate investments has been written down or reserved against pursuant to §210.6-21(f), describe the item and explain the basis for the write-down or reserve.

[6] State in a footnote to column E the aggregate cost for Federal income tax purposes.

[7] The amount of all intercompany profits included in the total of column E shall be stated if material.

[8] Summarize the aggregate amounts for each column applicable to captions 7 and 12 of §210.6-22.

[16 FR 348, Jan. 13, 1951, as amended at 16 FR 2655, Mar. 24, 1951. Redesignated at 45 FR 63679, Sept. 25, 1980]

§210.12-25 Supplementary profit and loss information.

Column A—Item[1]	Column B—Charged to investment expense	Column C—Charged to other accounts		Column D—Total
		(1)—Account	(2)—Amount	
1. Legal expenses (including those in connection with any matter, measure or proceeding before legislative bodies, officers or government departments)				
2. Advertising and publicity				
3. Sales promotion[2]				
4. Payments directly and indirectly to trade associations and service organizations, and contributions to other organizations				

[1] Amounts resulting from transactions with affiliates shall be stated separately.

[2] State separately each category of expense representing more than 5 percent of the total expense shown under this item.

§210.12-26 Certificate reserves.

Column A—Description[1]	Column B—Balance at beginning of period			Column C—Additions			Column D—Deductions			Column E—Balance at close of period		
	(1)—Number of accounts with security bidders	(2)—Amount of maturity value	(3)—Amount of reserved[2]	(1)—Charged to profit and loss or income	(2)—Reserve payments by certificate holders	(3)—Charged to other accounts describe	(1)—Maturities	(2)—Cash surenders prior to maturity	(3)—Other—describe	(1)—Number of accounts with security holders	(2)—Amount of maturity value	(3)—Amount of reserves[2]

[1] (a) Each series of certificates shall be stated separately. The description shall include the yield to maturity on an annual payment basis.

(b) For certificates of the installment type, information required by columns B, D (2) and (3) and E shall be given by age groupings, according to the number of months paid by security holders, grouped to show those upon which 1-12 monthly payments have been made, 13-24 payments, etc.

[2] (a) If the total of the reserves shown in these columns differs from the total of the reserves per the accounts, there should be stated (i) the aggregate difference and (ii) the difference on a $1,000 face-amount certificate basis.

(b) There shall be shown by footnote or by supplemental schedule (i) the amounts periodically credited to each class of security holders' accounts from installment payments and (ii) such other amounts periodically credited to accumulate the maturity amount of the certificate. Such information shall be stated on a $1,000 face-amount certificate basis for the term of the certificate.

§210.12-27 Qualified assets on deposit.[1]

Column A—Name of depositary[2]	Column B—Cash	Column C—Investments in securities	Column D—First mortgages and other first liens on real estate	Column E—Other	Column F—Total[3]

[1] All money columns shall be totaled.

[2] Classify names of individual depositaries under group headings, such as banks and states.

[3] Total of column F shall agree with note required by caption 11 of §210.6-22 as to total amount of qualified Assets on Deposit.

For certain real estate companies

§210.12-28   Real estate and accumulated depreciation.[1]
[For Certain Real Estate Companies]

Column A—Description[2]	Column B—Encumbrances	Column C—Initial cost to company		Column D—Cost capitalized subsequent to acquisition		Column E—Gross amount of which carried at close of period[3][4][5][6][7]			Column F—Accumulated depreciation	Column G—Date of construction	Column H—Date acquired	Column I—Life on which depreciation in latest income statements is computed
		Land	Buildings and improvements	Improvements	Carrying costs	Land	Buildings and improvements	Total				

[1] All money columns shall be totaled.

[2] The description for each property should include type of property (e.g., unimproved land, shopping center, garden apartments, etc.) and the geographical location.

[3] The required information is to be given as to each individual investment included in column E except that an amount not exceeding 5 percent of the total of column E may be listed in one amount as "miscellaneous investments."

[4] In a note to this schedule, furnish a reconciliation, in the following form, of the total amount at which real estate was carried at the beginning of each period for which income statements are required, with the total amount shown in column E:

Balance at beginning of period	$
Additions during period:	
Acquisitions through foreclosure	$
Other acquisitions	
Improvements, etc	
Other (describe)	$
Deductions during period:	
Cost of real estate sold	$
Other (describe)	
Balance at close of period	$

If additions, except acquisitions through foreclosure, represent other than cash expenditures, explain. If any of the changes during the period result from transactions, directly or indirectly with affiliates, explain the bases of such transactions and state the amounts involved.

A similar reconciliation shall be furnished for the accumulated depreciation.

[5] If any item of real estate investments has been written down or reserved against, describe the item and explain the basis for the write-down or reserve.

163

^{6} State in a note to column E the aggregate cost for Federal income tax purposes.

^{7} The amount of all intercompany profits included in the total of column E shall be stated if material.

[38 FR 6068, Mar. 6, 1983. Redesignated at 45 FR 63630, Sept. 25, 1980]

§210.12-29   Mortgage loans on real estate.[1]
[For Certain Real Estate Companies]

Column A—Description[2] [3] [4]	Column B—Interest rate	Column C—Final maturity date	Column D—Periodic payment terms[5]	Column E—Prior liens	Column F—Face amount of mortgages	Column G—Carrying amount of mortgages[3] [6] [7] [8] [9]	Column H—Principal amount of loans subject to delinquent principal or interest[10]

^{1} All money columns shall be totaled.

^{2} The required information is to be given for each individual mortgage loan which exceeds three percent of the total of column G.

^{3} If the portfolio includes large numbers of mortgages most of which are less than three percent of column G, the mortgages not required to be reported separately should be grouped by classifications that will indicate the dispersion of the portfolio, i.e., for a portfolio of mortgages on single family residential housing. The description should also include number of loans by original loan amounts (e.g., over $100,000, $50,000-$99,999, $20,000-$49,000, under $20,000) and type loan (e.g., VA, FHA, Conventional). Interest rates and maturity dates may be stated in terms of ranges. Data required by columns D, E and F may be omitted for mortgages not required to be reported individually.

^{4} Loans should be grouped by categories, e.g., first mortgage, second mortgage, construction loans, etc., and for each loan the type of property, e.g., shopping center, high rise apartments, etc., and its geographic location should be stated.

^{5} State whether principal and interest is payable at level amount over life to maturity or at varying amounts over life to maturity. State amount of balloon payment at maturity, if any. Also state prepayment penalty terms, if any.

^{6} In a note to this schedule, furnish a reconciliation, in the following form, of the carrying amount of mortgage loans at the beginning of each period for which income statements are required, with the total amount shown in column G:

Balance at beginning of period		$
Additions during period:		
New mortgage loans	$	
Other (describe)		$
Deductions during period:		
Collections of principal	$	
Foreclosures		
Cost of mortgages sold		
Amortization of premium		
Other (describe)		
Balance at close of period		$

If additions represent other than cash expenditures, explain. If any of the changes during the period result from transactions, directly or indirectly with affiliates, explain the bases of such transactions, and state the amounts involved. State the aggregate mortgages (a) renewed and (b) extended. If the carrying amount of new mortgages is in excess of the unpaid amount of the extended mortgages, explain.

[7] If any item of mortgage loans on real estate investments has been written down or reserved against, describe the item and explain the basis for the write-down or reserve.

[8] State in a note to column G the aggregate cost for Federal income tax purposes.

[9] The amount of all intercompany profits in the total of column G shall be stated, if material.

[10] (a) Interest in arrears for less than 3 months may be disregarded in computing the total amount of principal subject to delinquent interest.

(b) Of the total principal amount, state the amount acquired from controlled and other affiliates.

[38 FR 6069, Mar. 6, 1973; 38 FR 7323, Mar. 20, 1973. Redesignated at 45 FR 63680, Sept. 25, 1980]

Made in the USA
Middletown, DE
04 November 2021